British Columbia GAME FISH

*Dedicated to
the wives and lovers of sport fishermen.*

WESTERN FISH & GAME

British Columbia

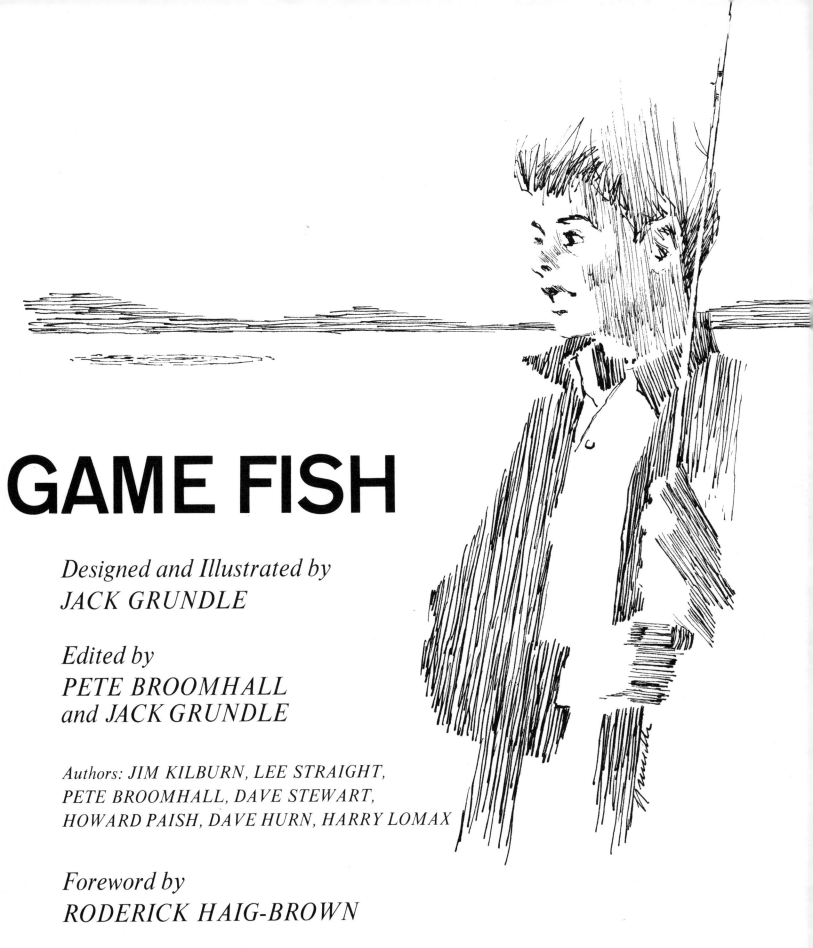

GAME FISH

Designed and Illustrated by
JACK GRUNDLE

Edited by
PETE BROOMHALL
and JACK GRUNDLE

Authors: JIM KILBURN, LEE STRAIGHT,
PETE BROOMHALL, DAVE STEWART,
HOWARD PAISH, DAVE HURN, HARRY LOMAX

Foreword by
RODERICK HAIG-BROWN

WESTERN FISH & GAME MAGAZINE LTD.
VANCOUVER, CANADA

LITHOGRAPHED IN CANADA LPIU 33L AGENCY PRESS LIMITED

FOREWORD

So far as I know, no one has ever attempted to make an exhaustive count of all the lakes and streams in British Columbia, but there are thousands, if not tens of thousands; most of them grow fish of one sort or another, and nearly all of those that do not could be made to. The variety of conditions is tremendous and the variety of fish stocks, developed by thousands of years of adaptation, is almost equally impressive. In addition to its fresh waters, the province has thousands of miles of coastline, deeply indented and usually more or less sheltered, as well as the enclosed minor sea of the Strait of Georgia, along which and in which the Pacific salmons and the steelhead trout migrate and feed. After more than a hundred years of white settlement, anglers — and biologists — are still only learning their way into this maze of possibilities.

It is true that some productive waters — and perhaps some valuable stocks — have already been damaged by over fishing, bad management, ill-conceived dams, pollution and other water abuses. Even to-day careless development of one sort or another is undoubtedly damaging some good fishing waters long before anglers in any numbers find them. All this makes the records and observations of anglers of real importance.

It is a happy thing to welcome a book such as this, which sets out in permanent form the views and theories and deeds of several of the most active, best-informed and keenest among British Columbia's angling brotherhood. It is a fine cross-section of special interests and, with Jack Grundle's lively illustrations, provides a good accounting of the state of development of the sport in British Columbia in the year 1970.

It is particularly interesting to notice that several of the authors make it clear that they have been fishing B.C. waters from childhood on. This means not only the development of home-grown talent — a pleasant manifestation in itself — but the development of life-time standards of comparison and with them a sense of proprietary rights. At first glance it may seem paradoxical to write of proprietary rights in a public resource, but it is not. The rights exist morally, if to an inadequate degree in law, and if they are not sensed and recognized there can be little hope of protecting them.

These authors proclaim them and to an important extent define them. There is, they say, a decline in quality. There has been a failure to step in and manage the fishery so that quality can be maintained. Some of the very best things, such as the runs of sea cutthroat and summer steelhead, may be fading away beyond recovery for lack of understanding and concern. The ubiquitous spinning reel and its effects in the form of increased pressure, though undoubtedly here to stay, have not been recognized by adequate regulations. Finally, and repeated in many forms, the careless encroachments of settlement and industry, endlessly debilitating, have not been named and contained.

This is a significant consensus. Even more significant is the recognition, often tacit but unmistakably there, that the time has come to develop standards and ethics in the sport itself in its many forms. No one in this book is fishing for meat or for bag limits or even for fish of record size. They are men concerned to go fishing in pleasant surroundings, under pleasant conditions, aiming to achieve only in accordance with their own ideas of what the standards should be.

Most of these men know much more than they have written here; most could have written a book as easily as a chapter or two, and no doubt some of them will. Lee Straight, probably the most widely experienced of British Columbia outdoor writers, has chosen to concentrate on chinook salmon fishing and has achieved an outstanding account of these splendid fish. Pete Broomhall is a link with Pintail, the late Jack Lillington, another of British Columbia's great outdoor columnists. Jim Kilburn may well be the first really solid expert on flyfishing for the trout of the interior lakes. And so it goes. It is a distinguished gathering, yet by no means oppressively so. The concern of each man is to reveal his sport, define the essence of it and carry the reader with him through the experience of it. In this, the writers are, without exception, perceptive, light-hearted and descriptive, unobsessed by technical details or pedantics. This is at once refreshing and, for the reader, richly rewarding.

It is a virtue of the book that new ways are examined and old fish, not always highly regarded, are re-assessed. Even exotics are considered with favor. It is true that the B.C. angler has been somewhat spoiled by the ready availability of first-rate game fish and has tended to disregard such interesting and rewarding species as whitefish and char. These and still others have their secure place in the future of the sport, but I think there is little need to despair of maintaining and in some cases restoring or increasing the old favorites.

The base of the fishing is in the clean water of snows and glaciers flowing over gravel beds through forested slopes to the sea. These nursed and reared the salmon stocks and much of the province's best fishing depends directly or indirectly on these. Ruthless and wasteful logging practices, conceived in ignorance, have done much damage, but there is also recovery through regrowth and one can hope that logging of future crops will be done with far greater care and consideration. Stream bed improvement, flow control and other techniques of modern management can take advantage of this renewal, and one can already see hope for rehabilitation of the salmon runs. The strengths and variety of the other native game-fish stocks should be sufficient, in many cases, to respond.

Of all the outdoor sports, fishing is the one most likely to persist. It has a wide and varied following, a true cross-section of the public. It is a gentle and artistic sport, with infinite scope for ingenuity, and associations that make for growth of the soul. Killing is not one of its essentials — as more and more sportsmen are discovering every day, fish can be released to swim away and there is often greater satisfaction in such release than in killing. Finally, the health of angling waters and the persistence of game fish species is one of the most accurate criteria of the health of a civilisation. If it is well with the waters and with the fish that live in them, it will be well with the people who live on the land.

RODERICK HAIG-BROWN

COLOUR ILLUSTRATIONS

CONTENTS

JIM KILBURN is a flyfisherman and a writer. And he's a perfectionist in both. He believes in intensity. And he intensely believes that mankind is too casual about quality fishing. His chapters on the *Rainbow Trout* and the *Cutthroat Trout* demonstrate Jim's regard for quality.

PETE BROOMHALL is a teacher. He was a professional outdoor writer. He thinks sport fishing is both a recreation and a re-creation. He values the past. He still wears thigh-high boots when he goes steelheading. Pete contributed the chapters on the *Pink Salmon*, the *Coho Salmon*, and the *Steelhead*.

LEE STRAIGHT is a well-known professional outdoor writer. He doesn't trust approximations or guesswork. He keeps a diary because he doesn't always trust his own memory. If he's not absolutely certain, he'll make certain. In his chapter on the *Chinook Salmon*, Lee tells it like it is.

DAVE STEWART is a non-stop outdoorsman. He probably spends more time fishing than he does at his home in Penticton. Next to fishing and exploring, he likes best to write about outdoor pursuits. Dave wrote the chapters on the *Whitefish*, the *Dolly Varden* and, the *Kokanee*.

HOWARD PAISH is a tireless outdoor enthusiast and conservationist. He has alerted British Columbians to many of the province's environmental problems. In his chapter, Howard alerts the reader to the sporting qualities of the *Eastern Brook Trout*.

DAVE HURN is a fishery biologist and angler. He views flyfishing as a contemplative undertaking, and as an art. He has successfully experimented with cast flies for coho salmon. His two daughters are trollers. His son is a beginning flyfisher. Dave contributed the chapter on the *Brown Trout*.

HARRY LOMAX is a resident of Prince George. He fishes extensively throughout northern British Columbia. He is convinced that the province's north is God's country. It is natural that Harry should write the chapters on the *Lake Trout* and the *Arctic Grayling*.

Rainbow Trout

Chinook Salmon

Steelhead Trout

Coho Salmon

18

Coastal Cutthroat Trout

Brown Trout

22

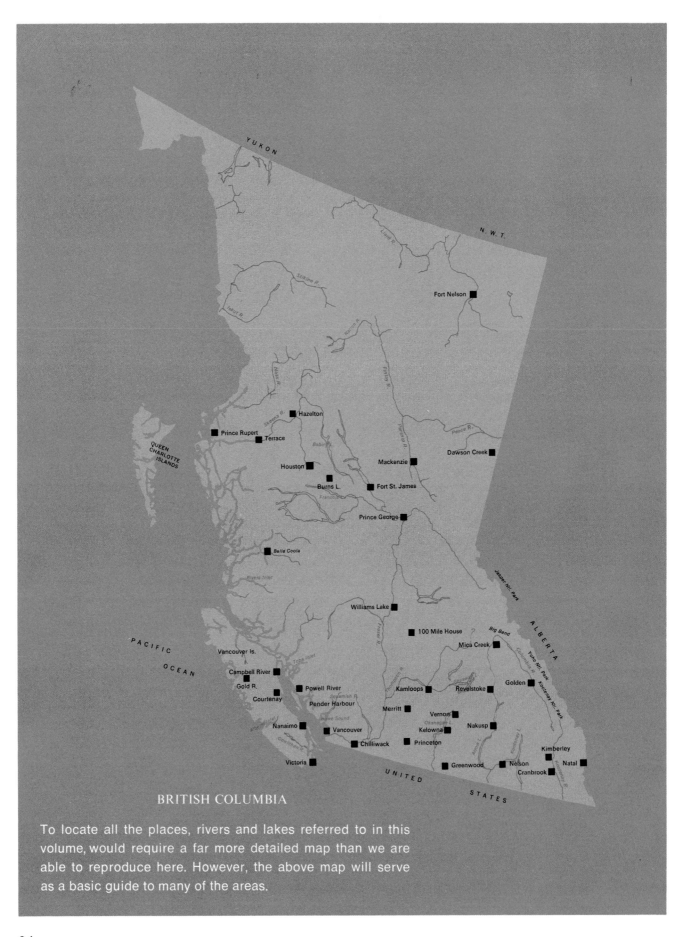

YUKON

N. W. T.

Liard R.

Stikine R.

Fort Nelson

Iskut R.

Nass R.

Finlay R.

Peace R.

Hazelton

Skeena R.

Prince Rupert

Terrace

Babine L.

Dawson Creek

QUEEN CHARLOTTE ISLANDS

Houston

Mackenzie

Burns L.

Fort St. James

Francois L.

Prince George

Bella Coola

Rivers Inlet

Jasper Ntl. Park

ALBERTA

Williams Lake

100 Mile House

Big Bend

Fraser R.

Mica Creek

Columbia R.

Yoho Ntl. Park

PACIFIC

Vancouver Is.

OCEAN

Toba Inlet

Campbell River

Kamloops

Revelstoke

Golden

Kootenay Ntl. Park

Gold R.

Powell River

Squamish R.

Courtenay

Pender Harbour

Merritt

Vernon

Howe Sound

Okanagan L.

Nakusp

Nanaimo

Vancouver

Kelowna

Chilliwack

Princeton

Kimberley

Victoria

Greenwood

Nelson

Natal

UNITED

Cranbrook

STATES

BRITISH COLUMBIA

To locate all the places, rivers and lakes referred to in this
volume, would require a far more detailed map than we are
able to reproduce here. However, the above map will serve
as a basic guide to many of the areas.

24

British Columbia GAME FISH

Jim Kilburn

The Coastal Cutthroat Trout

Nostalgia is not the private privilege of the angler, but in a rapidly-wasting world the angler has an uncommon right to dwell in the past. There are thousands of anglers in this the province of the good life who would gladly swap the glib life for a chance to turn back the clock. They quite naturally yearn for the Golden Past of one short generation ago. In those idyllic days, there were many quiet, unmarred stretches of streams and lakes where a flyfisher could cast for trout. In those days, the trout fisher was too complacent. And today, it may already be too late. Unfortunately, much of British Columbia's sport fishing is already relegated to history. And so it is that when I think about sea-run cutthroats, I often hearken back to an autumn day six years ago when a telephone call from my fishing partner kindly rescued me from a thankless task of backyard weed-pulling.

Over the years I have noticed that when fishing partners phone, they can be most irritating. Martin Tolley was no different. On this occasion, he even sounded a wee bit smug. But he had difficulty subduing his excitement; it was there in the undertone:

"James, whatever are you up to? You're wheezing like a pilot model of the Stanley Steamer."

It would have done me no good to come right out and say "You don't even know what a Stanley is never mind what a Steamer was, so don't give me any of your damn-quick similes." The politic way of wheedling information from Tolley-types calls for an innocent, or even a down-right disinterested, pose.

"Just working in the garden. And how's the world treating you?" (Bland, but the question calls for an answer.)

"Oh, not too badly. I merely wanted to mention having had some good sport with cutthroat as long as your arm."

Silence.

In the gamesmanship of telephone talk, that pause put Martin one up on me. And he knew it. I lost my poise.

"All right, never mind acting so damned smug. Tell me all about it. Don't just gloat."

"My, my," Martin mused. "Who was it who said that gardening was good for the soul; or did he say soil?"

"Now you listen to me, Martin . . ."

"Okay, okay. Indeed I did have some excellent fish; I shall say nothing of aching wrists, snapped tippets, or masticated flies. Nor shall . . ."

"Hold on," I interrupted, "Where did you say this happened?"

"I didn't, James old boy, I didn't."

Another pause. But this time I outwaited him.

"I'd be happy to squire you on a repeat venture," Martin continued, "provided you can tear yourself away from your cabbages and cauliflowers, and provided . . ."

"Yes?" I begged.

"Provided you take me to that pet coho hole of yours, the one you've alluded to so many times—you know, where they pile up like cordwood and grab flies like crazy."

Martin had been trying to worm that piece of information out of me for some time. And now he had me. We both knew it.

"Deal," I submitted.

Early the next morning, we took a car ferry to the promised land. At about half past nine, we turned off the main road. We wound down the steep, gravelled road, clattered over the decking that bridged a tiny stream, and came to a halt.

It was one of those bleak, misty days of early October. Although damp, it was a warm and pleasant day, and we were in good spirits. We followed the wooded trail that alternately met and departed from the tiny stream. The stream was full of Chum salmon. Some were spawning; others were thrusting upstream in search of less crowded spawning gravel.

Here and there, grouse erupted from the undergrowth. Above the autumn-colored canopy, scarcely visible crows scolded us for intruding. All was right with the world.

Soon we emerged on to a beautifully serene beach. The still-ebbing tide had bared a wide strip of marsh grass. The small stream, as if suddenly more anxious to reach the sea, fairly rushed through an eel-grass flat. Beyond the creek-mouth, sea and sky merged in the morning mist. The wooded crest of an island seemed to float on the stark silhouettes of an offshore log-boom.

Diving fowl patrolled between log-boom and beach, and at the water's edge, sandpipers dipped and scurried at their morning business.

A profusion of springtide logs lay tightly packed in a narrow band along the foreshore's entire length. The gnarled roots of half-buried deadheads spread darkly amid the lighter golds and greens of the marsh grass.

To the left, several weathered shacks perched greyly along the edge of a small, marshy bay. To the right, there was more marsh, then a shoreline-timbered cove that had a sharply sloped sand and pebble beach. Martin had already named these spots Left and Right bays.

At his suggestion, we started for Left Bay. We walked leisurely over the barnacled shells of oysters and clams, occasionally pausing to watch for signs of trout. On one such occasion, Martin pointed toward some tiny dimples that were barely discernible on the glass-smooth surface.

"One never knows with sea-runs, does one? But that looks like herring, and where there's herring, there should be a cutthroat or two. Try just out from the old shacks; that's where I had my best luck yesterday."

Somewhat suspicious of so much goodwill, I half watched Martin as I tied on a number eight American Coachman. A nearby and loud splash broke the spell. I quickly looked up to see wavelets spreading from a surface swirl. Duck or trout? There was only one way to find out. I quickly dropped the Coachman close to the swirl, began to retrieve the fly in fast strips, and was as quickly treated to the sight of a bulging wave following my fly. I stopped my retrieve to watch the flyline. The line twitched—once, twice. I raised the rod point, and slowly tightened. The fish was suddenly on, and suddenly in the air. He made three clean leaps, then settled down to a strong, subsurface struggle. Although he seldom took line, he seldom yielded it either—for the first several minutes. He simply cruised stubbornly up and down the shoreline shallows. On several occasions I unsuccessfully attempted to turn him onto the beach. But finally, as all fish must, he weakened. It was a sudden surrender when it came. And he was as handsome a fish as an angler has any right to expect: heavily spotted, lightly touched with a lemon-yellow tint, smoothly fat, and four pounds. I gently slipped the fly from the corner of his jaw, held him quietly in ankle-deep water till he recovered, then watched him swim slowly out to sea, apparently none the worse for his experience.

For the next hour, the sea-runs came eagerly to the Coachman. Down the beach to my right, Martin was enjoying similar good fortunes. Then the tide changed, and with the flooding tide came a marked change in the cutthroats' behaviour. They no longer took firmly; they followed only half-heartedly, and merely plucked at the fly. Soon even the plucking ended.

Martin waved me over. After comparing results, Martin suggested that Right Bay might now be ripe. On a previous trip, he had found Right Bay to be the right place during the latter stages of a flooding tide.

I soon discovered that Right Bay was not easily fished. The beach sloped sharply from the forest edge for thirty or forty feet, then levelled off. By the time there would be enough water to cover the fish, there would also be little room for backcasts. Nevertheless, we patiently waited for the tide to fill the bay. We waited for perhaps one hour as the tide inched in. Then, as Martin had predicted, a cutthroat swirled. He was well out in the bay. But moments later, another swirled, and this one was barely beyond casting range.

That was the signal we needed. Because of the slope, we could only wade a short distance from shore, and we could not lay out as much line as we would have liked. However, we had made only exploratory casts before Martin's rod tip suddenly dipped sharply. Once again we began to catch trout, and for a short period we enjoyed superb sport. But the tide waits for no man, not even ardent flyfishers; too soon we were forced so far shoreward that it was virtually impossible to continue casting. When we left, the cutthroats were still swirling and dimpling in the calm grey sea.

Over the years, Martin and I have stumbled onto several other trouty bays and beaches. Some were even more beautiful. But none was more generous than Right and Left Bays. We had four good seasons there. We caught many of the big sea-run cutthroat that lived there, but we killed few of them. We hoped that those magnificent fish would be there for many seasons to come. And then, on an autumn day of a new season, we found that our concern had been for nothing.

The clapboard bridge crossing the small stream was the same as ever, but the once-beautifully wooded trail was now an ugly bulldozed road; at one point the creek was now squeezed into a concrete culvert over which was an earth-filled bridge; and the lower reaches of the creek now spilled through a wasteland tangle of slash and uprooted trees that reached down to the tidal flats. In the name of progress, such things and more are done. One season later, a wharf jutted obscenely over the flats of Right Bay; and along the entire shoreline, sprawled right at the high-water mark, was a tightly-packed network of log-booms.

The trout might still be there, if one cares to look for them. And perhaps, when the tide is extremely high, there might even be enough water in which to work a fly. But the booms have not only shrunk the fishing space, they have also scoured and rutted the once-natural shoreline. It is no longer a place for the flyfisher.

And in the name of progress, man is as rapidly ruining other good cutthroat trout haunts. Only last season a beach was bulldozed, an estuary was rerouted, and a beachfront was piledriven with toxic-arsenate treated logs. It is little wonder both that the angler must look further afield for his sport, and that the once-numerous sea-run cutthroat is already scarce.

Last autumn, friends and I who admire the sea-runs searched for and found a yet-unspoiled cutthroat beach. It is perhaps the most beautiful and trouty spot we have ever discovered. It is not a typical tidal beach; it has no marsh grass, sloughs or mud flats. It is a gently-sloping beach of small, clean gravel. The sea waters that wash it are crystal clean. And, on certain phases of the tide, it is patrolled by schools of magnificent cutthroat trout. We call it Pebble Beach.

For the time being, Pebble Beach seems safely hidden from the cold, searching eyes of progress. Perhaps Pebble Beach will provide several seasons of good sport. Perhaps. But no matter for how many autumns it remains unspoiled, I will never be able to go there without dreading that I will see the signs that precede destruction—the surveyor's ribbons and pegs. When I see those tell-tale signs, I will be saddened, and I will once again be searching.

One day, there may be no unspoiled areas to search for, and there may be no more cutthroat trout. And then the end will be written to another chapter in the history of the decline and fall of B.C. sport fishing. And then, too, there will be no future. There will only be the past. And nostalgia. For everyone.

ANYONE WHO has ever met a coastal cutthroat knows him as a handsome fish. Many, myself included, believe him to be the most attractive game fish of the Pacific Coast. I, for one, like the cutthroat whether his sides are shiny silver or lemon-yellow, or whether his fins are transparent white or orange-rimmed. And I like to meet these heavily-spotted trout on drizzly winter days, and on glittering summer afternoons. To me, the coastal cutthroat is the trout for all seasons.

The cutthroat was probably so named because he often wears two slash-like marks on the underside of his jaw. On some, the slashes are bright red; on others, the marks are quite faint. Whether it is of jaw, fin, or side, the coloration of cutthroat trout varies considerably. He also varies in other ways. A hooked cutthroat sometimes runs hard and jumps often; he sometimes struggles doggedly and stays submerged. Sometimes a mature cutthroat weighs mere ounces; sometimes he weighs more than fifteen pounds. Sometimes he takes an angler's offerings with suicidal abandon; sometimes he perversely refuses everything.

Although the cutthroat is native only to the Pacific Coast of North America, he inhabits both fresh and salt water, and his range is extensive—from Northern California to Southern Alaska. Like so many salmon and trout, the cutthroat matures and spawns in his fourth year. And like his other freshwater relatives, he needs unpolluted creeks and rivers in which to spawn and grow. Like so many game fish, he faces extinction unless measures are taken to curb pollution. And like other trout, cutthroat occasionally spawn more than once, sometimes several times.

Quite naturally, cutthroat that take up housekeeping in the rivers and streams of coastal British Columbia generally tend to be smallish. After all, B.C.'s coastal lakes and streams are not rich in fish food. However, there are large coastal lakes where cutthroat grow to a most respectable size indeed. Two such renowned lakes are Sproat, on Vancouver Island, and Powell, near the mainland pulpmill port of Powell River.

Many theories have been offered as to why cutthroats vary so much in size. Genetics has been suggested, and it has been proven that big trout beget big eggs, and that big eggs beget big, healthy trout. And so on. Carried on long enough, it is possible that a strain of large, superbly-conditioned (man-attacking?) trout would evolve. But although big trout are generally more aggressive, and consequently better fed and healthier than are smaller trout of the same age class, the growth rate of coastal cutthroat is largely a result of the quantity and quality of the available food supply.

Most coastal rivers and streams are poor producers of fish food for two primary reasons: the nutrient content of the water is too low, and fluctuations of both stream-flow and water temperature are too high. Coastal lakes, though relatively barren, are more stable, and hence richer in planktonic life. Such lakes are more suitable for permanent and semi-permanent populations of forage-type fishes such as sticklebacks and salmon and trout fry. In turn, these fishes form a considerable part of the lake cutthroat's diet, and hence are a primary reason why lake cutthroats grow to greater sizes than do their river cousins.

Further, there is a good chance that the more stable conditions of the coastal lakes also result in both a higher survival of spawned trout and an increase in the size of individual spawners. I say individual spawners because the growth rate of spawned fish seldom compares with that of maiden trout. Kelts, particularly consecutive-year spawners, seldom fully recover from the spawning ordeal. But, a proportion of multiple-spawning cutthroat do not spawn every year, but every other year. Such trout, though few, would likely be the largest specimens of any lake's cutthroat population.

Though primarily a freshwater trout, the coastal cutthroat may develop anadromous tendencies during any year of its freshwater life. It will then abandon its parent stream for a nomadic life in the sea. Like its freshwater brother, the growth rate of saltwater cutthroat also varies according to food supply. However, it is the year in which the cutthroat migrates to sea that more accurately determines his size at maturity. Sea-runs that leave their parent streams early in the second year are generally bigger at maturity than are those that leave in their third, fourth, or fifth years. The early migrant becomes bigger simply because he gets a longer shot at the richer seafood diet.

The story of coastal cutthroat size is made more complex by the fact that the size of migrants in any given year also ranges considerably. There are a number of reasons for variation in migrant size, not the least of which is the behaviour patterns of individual specimens. It seems fairly certain that some saltwater cutthroat travel little during their entire life. Others leave their parent streams early in life, and make periodic raids into freshwater to take advantage of temporary abundances—such as salmon eggs, salmon fry, or insects. Some make excursions into the open ocean, and apparently feed well for their trouble. All in all, it is not surprising that sea-runs frequently vary from about one to eight pounds when mature. Much seems to depend on whether the trout was an early- or late-comer to sea life, and whether he was a beach- or an ocean-feeding trout.

Even though the approximately-three-month-long spawning season does not begin until February, some mature sea-run cutthroat begin their upstream migration as early as July. Such cutthroat usually belong to moder-ately large streams, or rivers. Other sea-runs, particularly those of small creeks, stay in the sea until the very last moment. Many ready-to-spawn cutthroat have been encountered in tidal waters as late as February.

Unfortunately, few sea-runs seem to survive the spawning ordeal. It would appear that a high percentage of the spawned-out trout that return to the sea later succumb to the rigors of the fresh-to-saltwater transition. Others are likely easier-than-usual prey for marine predators such as seal, ling cod, and dog fish.

And, as if the cutthroat did not face enough pressures from the growing human population—the pressures of pollution and other misuses of water being foremost—I am convinced that the sea-run cutthroat populations can be seriously depleted by over-harvesting. (And I am aware that some biologists may deny this claim, but they are merely guessing too. The simple truth is that no one knows; the sea-run cutthroat is basically an unstudied fish). Perhaps it is unfortunate that the sea-run is relatively easy to catch. But, fortunately, it is possible for those who don't measure the trout's value in pounds and ounces to attempt to safeguard their sport. They can briefly admire, then release the fish that provide such valuable moments.

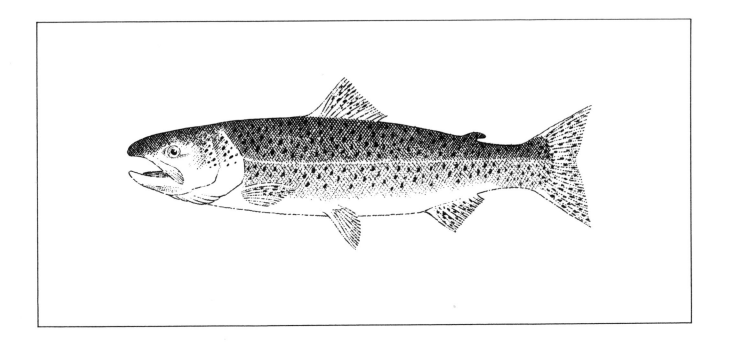

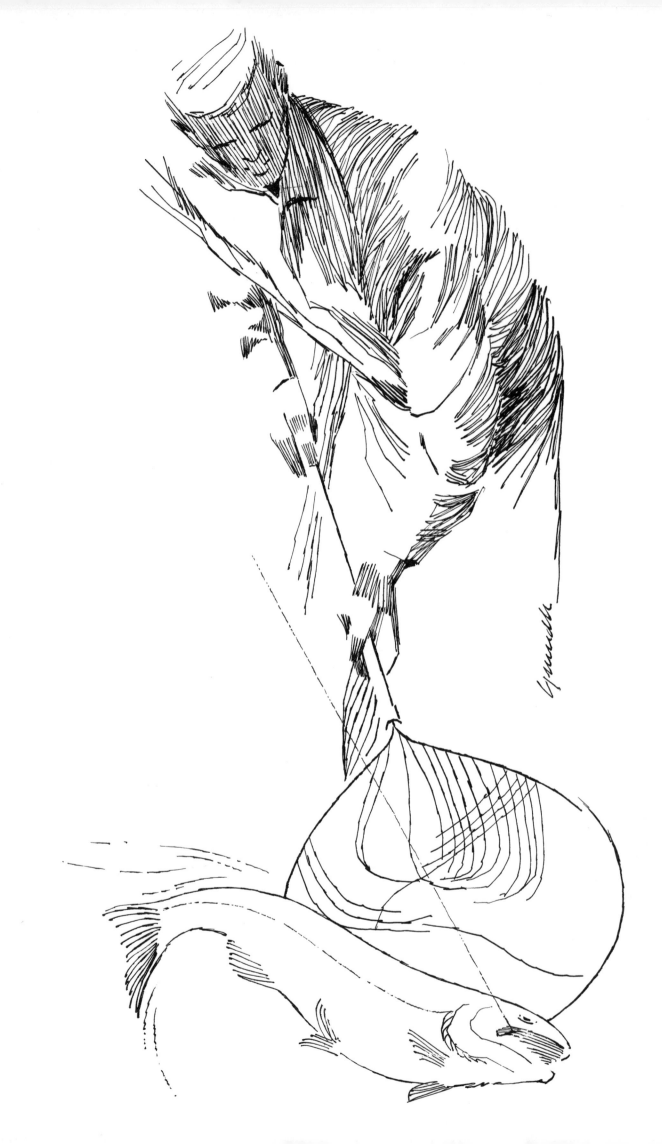

Lee Straight

The Chinook Salmon

THE SCHOOL of chinook salmon had hovered there all day like grey ghosts in the murk among the crags that push up through the black, sandy ooze of the floor of Sargeant Bay. As the late afternoon shadow began to spread across the entrance to the bay, a stocky, silver-bright salmon rose from the school. It was just under the arbitrary 30-pound tyee size. Its great, square tail swished it easily through a broad band of bright water and slanted it up, up into the shadow of a 10-foot boulder along the shore.

The strapping salmon circled grandly and sidled into the new lie. Its pectoral fins paddling, it brushed carelessly past several barely visible filaments that stretched down from the surface, 25 feet above, to near the bottom. The slim strands were held there by almost identical, crescent-shaped torpeodoes of lead, swivel-equipped at each end, weighing one or two ounces. Each sinker was worried by a live herring about seven inches long, tethered by six- or seven-foot wisps of leader. In turn, each fish wore a chrome-plated treble hook with one prong pushed into one nostril and out the other; another treble hook stuck into the skin of the herring's back or side.

The 28-pound chinook, an immaculate, unscarred cock fish, could see dozens of those cobwebs in the distant, bright, sun-bathed water and, above them, dozens of boat bottoms of all sizes and shapes. It wasn't concerned enough, however, to take alarm and abandon the area. Some boats moved along slowly, their propellors also beating slowly at their sterns. Some had oars dipping or hanging at each side. Most were nearly motionless in location but agitated by movement within, tethered to anchor lines that ended in the murky sand and rocks of the bay floor.

The chinook hadn't fed since he had almost munched his way into Sargeant Bay shortly after dawn. With his several dozen schoolmates he had followed a great school of herring in its wanderings west from Davis Bay, past Sechelt, just as wolves daily rove along the outskirts of vast caribou herds in the north. Accustomed to high living, our fish was abnormally fat and solid, hovering between a condition of great beauty (to the angler) and downright obesity. To achieve and maintain such bulk he usually was first to leave his own school and venture into the brightness. The chinook (*Oncorhynchus tshawytscha*) tends to avoid brightness more than does any other of the five species of Pacific salmon of the Oncorhynchus genus.

Already he was slightly head-high and keening for sight, or sound, of the mixed school of herring and anchovies he had watched lackadaisically crisscrossing the deeps of the bay all day, worried-at by dogfish and coho salmon and the occasional bottom fish that darted up from the blackness to envelop any remaining prey that had been injured but still went unnoticed. Cohoes feed any hour of the day. The school of bait fish appeared, stretching about 200 feet by 100, shaped liked a diamond, the upper fish only six feet beneath the glowing ceiling of their aquatic "room," the deepest part of the school parting to avoid the rocks of the steep shoreline.

Impatient with hunger, the chinook rushed the front of the school which scattered and easily avoided him in the good visibility beyond the shadow whence he burst like a fishy fullback. As the surprisingly agile salmon swirled back, black gums and strong teeth showing, to snap up expected casualties, he saw only one herring that appeared in trouble and closed his pointed jaws upon it, crosswise. Then he expectorated it to swallow it nose first to slip down more easily. They don't chew their food. As he spat it, he felt a tiny scratch and the hardness of the bait's nose hook. He sensed the unnaturalness, which made him swerve instinctively an inch or so to one side at the last split second of the grab.

Above, alone in a mere toy of a boat, a car-top pram of less than eight feet, sat an alert Sechelt resident, wiser than most of the other 100 or more anglers drawn to the bay by the recent good fishing reports. This man had learned that that point had features that seemed to attract early-feeding salmon. He was only in his late twenties but already a veteran at "mooching" bait on light tackle. He was looking right at the rod whose tip jiggled to the motion of the live herring bait trying to dodge the first passage of the voracious salmon below. Instantly the angler was hovering, vulture-like, hands poised over the rod, as it nodded, then bowed deep when the leader was brushed and the herring hooks slightly snagged. The salmon might have gone unscathed but for the keenness of the hook points and the short reaction time of that devoted young angler. One abrupt snatch-and-heave of the 11-foot rod, the man's arms stretched violently aloft like a terrified holdup victim's, had snapped the bait and its pair of treble hooks back into the outside of the gill plate or "cheek" of the great chinook. He was instantly and firmly hooked.

Then started another of the British Columbia replays of Ernest Hemingway's *The Old Man and the Sea*, with one of our unpredictable chinook salmon standing in for the Cuban bluefin tuna of Hemingway's epic. The ensuing see-saw was unusual but not rare among chinook salmon encounters. The fish turned and dashed south toward the Trail Islands, taking about 700 feet of nylon monofilament from the gutty angler's new single-action, fly-type, sea-reel before it slowed and turned to let him reel in his second line, take up the oars and scull after his intended prey. He didn't have to row again. The fish towed him into the light breeze. It wasn't pricked painfully but, being tethered by the outside of its head, well back of the snout, it had more command of the situation than usual. It didn't tire. It seemed to become bored.

Several times it allowed the angler to regain most of his line, then saw or heard the boat and dashed another 300 or 400 feet. The rests between the dashes were just as nerve-wracking because the leader test-strength was only 12 pounds. The throb of the huge fish's tail was always there, up through the line, down through the long, limber rod to the very butt as it cruised below, testing the contours of Trail Bay into which it eventually swam, two miles from the fishing fleet.

Almost three dozen fish were hooked and about half of them boated that evening, all but one on still-fished or drifted live baits, that odd one on a trolled plug. The rest of the salmon school had grown bolder with the fading light. At sundown of the early July evening, several reels buzzed and several rods were simultaneously tight-bowed. The action slowed at dark and all boats left, some roaring west to Halfmoon Bay, others going straight ashore to the tent-trailer camp.

Against the last wisp of red-gold sunset, however, there still bobbed that little car-top pram. Its passenger was a sturdy man, a good swimmer and a veteran of the outdoors. He knew every curve of the shoreline, even much of the marine chart by memory. But he was in a limbo between heaven and hell. He would not have relinquished his place for anything under a tidy sum of money or a better boat, tackle and place to fish. He shivered occasionally, more with the tension than with the sharpening night air, almost an intoxication. He also appreciated that a night wind could put him into trouble.

He calculated and shrugged at the risk of being far out in Trail Bay at night in a tiny plywood coracle with no extra floatation, only his life-jacket. Mainly he feared that the light wind would freshen and swing into the west, forcing him to cut and run. The man was a loner. He had a week's layoff from work. No one knew where he had gone so he might not be missed for days.

He finally teased his sinker to the rod-tip just at day-break, almost 12 hours after he hooked the chinook. It took another 25 minutes, with his arms now so cramped and tired, to edge the slab of a fish across his huge landing net.

The angler lay across the net handle to rest a moment, then dragged the net and bulky trophy carefully, desperately, over the boat gunwale. His triumph was dampened by disappointment in the actual weight of the fish. He gasped at its beauty, but couldn't help exclaiming aloud over the fact that it wasn't twice the weight. It took over an hour to scull back to the beach at the head of Sargeant Bay where few anglers were up and about. There is comparatively little morning action in that fishery, unusual for chinook salmon Meccas, so the angler had only half a dozen admiring stares as he unloaded then toted his boat to his pickup truck.

He didn't bother explaining that he'd not just gone out that dawn for the fish. He was almost as meek about taking so long over a 28-pounder as he was proud of just catching such a salmon at all. He did borrow another spring scale to verify his own and it matched the weight within a pound. Sargeant Bay chinooks, being feeders enroute elsewhere, are weeks from maturity and are an average-sized race of fish. Anything over 25 pounds is an outstanding catch there. The angler needn't have been apologetic about his lack of despatch. I recall an even longer fight, also at Sargeant Bay and also with that light tackle, but with two men spelling off one another from a large launch where they could mug-up with coffee and all. They took 14 hours to subdue a 31-pounder.

Then there was a very early morn, one August-end, when two Vancouver anglers, one experienced in that specific fishery, both well travelled outdoorsmen, rented an inboard "putt-putt" at Comox. Equipped with three light trolling rods, they felt their way through the dark with perhaps 40 other boats, across to the tyee pool at Royston just south of the Courtenay-Puntledge River-mouth drop-off. They would be trolling salmon plugs about 30 feet behind six-ounce sinkers, dropped in turn just a few feet below the nodding rod-tips. They sought the finning, fretting tyee chinooks that pause for days at the drop-off before dropping river temperatures lure

them into the river to the spawning ground where they had been born. The more experienced man had learned local techniques from fishing guides on a few trips, then chose to fish without them thereafter. He was an outdoors writer who had reported occasionally on the fine fishing found there.

The writer trolled a chrome-plated, hollow brass plug on his ultra-light center rod, its tip rested alongside the boat tiller, the butt of the rod lying on the floor. His reel was unusual in Vancouver Island circles, except among the many visiting U.S. anglers. It was a small, level-wind, star-drag, sea-reel holding 100 yards of 18-pound-test plastic monofilament line (a manufacturer's sample, no doubt) and 200 more yards of 15- to 20-pound-test backing line. The other two rods held British single-action reels and 200 or 300 yards of 20- to 25-pound-test line.

Everything promised a good weekend. While the actions of a hooked chinook are the least predictable of all British Columbia sport fish, and their at-sea peregrinations not easy to forecast, their schedule around their home streams near spawning time is accurately predictable. Their feeding habits, or the periods when they notice fishing lures, run almost exactly to a pattern by tide and moon. The writer had learned from reports and his own scattered adventures among chinooks that they "home" on the upper Vancouver Island rivers of both coasts during August, reaching peak populations at the river-mouths in early September. He also had learned from Campbell River, Comox and Cowichan anglers that the tides that bring on the greatest tyee activity, at least in respect to angling, were the low slacks and the ensuing flood, starting just before daybreak. Chinooks, being shy and verging on the nocturnal, like to lurk in shadow, avoiding surface waters in full daylight. The river estuary shallows betray their presence more than the open sea, but they still move more extensively in the early morning flood tides. There was a low slack tide 30 minutes before dawn that Saturday morning, and the weather was overcast but calm and mild; hence the promising outlook. Anglers arriving the previous evening were greeted with news of several catches despite light fishing activity Friday.

Just as the dawn blush began to show what was causing the nearby putt-putting, whirring, clanking, chuckles, splashes and the odd curse, our writer's middle reel buzzed. He'd glanced first at the side rods, baited with the so-called "pink-pearl" but actually almost white plugs, which more often draw attention in the first moments of the day. In fact, he had pointedly assigned the two side rods to his partner-guest, trolling that third, very light outfit just to be more efficient. But it was the chrome-plated plug that was drawing off the line.

It could have been snagged on the eel grass of the shallow river flats. It was easy to edge too far inshore in efforts to avoid the congestion. The writer turned and lifted the rod, threw on a little more drag by pressing the tips of the drag star away from him, then jerked the rod for any sign of life. There was life, all right. Not 60 feet astern, almost at the gunwhale of a following boat, surfaced a sturdy looking salmon, the big chrome lure glinting in its maw.

"My gawd, it's a fish all right," said the reporter, then proffered the rod to his partner. "Keep it," said the latter, a long stretch forward on the bow thwart.

It proved a typical encounter in that tight-packed fishery. The salmon went under two other boats but both craft rode harmlessly over the taut line. They were inboards, their propellors inset above keel skegs, long metal straps that slid over the gossamer line without so much as bruising it. Those were the only tense moments of the encounter until they came to boat the fish. The tyee chugged right out of the fishing fleet, the boat putting after it as soon as the partner reeled in the other two lines and stowed the rods. The fish took out only 400 feet of line, just beyond the monofilament, in its one long easy dash, then was merely testy, shaking its head often, in the ensuing tug-o'-war. It was writhing on their gaffhook in 10 minutes and beat out its real protest by threatening to drum its way through the floorboards.

It proved large enough, much larger than the men expected.

"I've had 20-pounders do better," said the writer. "You know," confided his partner, "I haven't looked over many tyees since I lived over here as a boy, but that appears a sizable salmon to me."

"Perhaps," said the tour leader. "It's my first tyee trip of the year so I can only guess it at over 40 pounds. A stocky fish." By the time their boat returned to the fleet 20 minutes later, other fish were being played. Sport appeared as good as they dared hope. They had hardly lowered their lures again before the same plug was roughly snatched up by a salmon, the rod quickly thrust upon the bow angler and a more usual and exciting Comox salmon tussle experienced. Though it was a smaller fish, handled by an angler who had battled many, and though the boat followed it under power, it took almost 20 minutes to bring to gaff.

They hooked and lost two more fish before the action tailed off about 9 a.m., their third and fourth striking a pearl pink plug. Back at the Comox wharf the two fish were weighed in by the local tyee club for award buttons.

Our anglers were astounded to find the gentler tyee to be an amazing 65½ pounds, a diamond button-fish, an angler's lifetime top trophy. It proved the best that season at Comox and second only to a 68-pounder from Campbell River for Vancouver Island's best of the year (1960). It ranked third only to a Kitimat River tyee in the annual *Field and Stream* magazine awards. Yet it was boated in 10 minutes. Their other fish was respectable enough, a 32-pound bronze button-winner.

The morning's tally in the tyee pool was 14 fish. Three more were reported taken in the evening "bite," usually a slower time. The next day a storm blew up, keeping most boats ashore but allowing three tyees to be taken by the few boats that slipped straight out from the Royston shore. The bulk of that run of fish rode the high tides into the rain-swollen Puntledge River the next two or three days, and the season was almost over for another year.

THE FOREGOING TWO ANECDOTES are examples of the extreme variability of the fishery for the northwest's most enigmatic sport fish. Coho anglers, preferring the greater number of encounters and the surface fighting; and steelhead trouters, preferring rivers to sea or lake, might smile behind their hands at the thought of comparing their champions with the chinook. As one who has sought all those fish for almost five decades, this observer hastens to explain.

River-trouting *is* special and precious and grows ever more rare. Cohoes *are* rambunctious, hook-spitting leapers, while chinooks leap less but last longer—much longer as a rule—and smash more tackle. I enjoy all three sports and actually spend more time on cohoes and steelhead, but none of the salmonids strikes me as more handsome than the massive, bronze-gold cock tyee just doffing his silver for his spawning colors; or the steely-blue, deep-bodied bar of silvery muscle that is the immature chinook, perhaps 10, often 35 pounds in active feeding and fighting trim, whether from beneath the polluted waters that wash harbor piling or from the sparkling rapids of the Skookumchuck, Yuculta, Discovery Passage or Active Pass. If one relishes sea-food, can he find anywhere in the world a red-fleshed fish that surpasses the flavor of the red chinook (or of the white-fleshed variety if one wears a blindfold)?

As for challenges involved, the very skill needed to take the chinook rates him a number one game fish. Certainly there are easily-taken chinooks. All salmon have their suicidal types when they swarm in plenty. The art lies first in finding salmon or trout then in presenting lure or

bait squarely before him, rather than merely "fooling" it.

No other salmon or trout is taken so extensively as the chinook—from the far-flung corners of the North Pacific Coast, any day in the year, on so many rigs at so many depths, or so far up the rivers. The chinook is an all-weather, all-tackle sport fish. If it were more numerous it would monopolize our sea fishing interest, shared even now only with the coho.

The chinook is best known to tourists in its tyee state. Tyee is an Indian word meaning chieftain and, while likely applied to the chinook to dub it the king of salmon, now applies to those chinooks topping the 30-pound mark, an arbitrary minimum weight for club button awards. The tyee fisheries are usually near their home rivermouths, occasionally in the upper reaches of some large rivers. Otherwise, it is not a fish whose best season suits the tourist. That characteristic, along with its shyness, may be its very salvation. The most productive time for chinooks, in success per fishing hour, is in winter. If one will dress warmly enough to keep comfortable while sitting still for hours, one can find good chinook sport from the southern extremity of its range, off San Francisco, to its northern limits, the Aleutian Islands. Far more of these chinooks are captured as bright, firm immatures in winter, spring and early summer, than as the darker, more indolent "tyees" of the rivermouth pool, or as river-runs.

Commencing in October and increasingly in November, the young chinook varies from a half-pound "grilse," which are smolts just out of the rivers, up to about ten pounds—all sizes increasing rapidly. Also commonly caught through the winter are the previous year's grilse, fish that will mature rapidly enough to become the ensuing season's mature fish. These are three to six pounds in December, six to 20 pounds by the following May, June or July.

Scientists once believed almost all chinooks dwelt in their home streams a year or two after birth, then silvered-up and eased backwards down to sea as smolts roaming the Pacific another year, two or three, to return most often as four-year-olds, sometimes as three or fives. They know that the fry of some chinook races, particularly those of shorter rivers, also may enter the sea a few days, or perhaps a few weeks after they leave the river gravel as free-swimming fry, the later migrants being less numerous but enjoying a higher survival rate. Races of chinooks that commonly reach the over-30-pound proportions are generally four to seven years of age, spending those extra years in their marine roaming.

Tagging and oceanographic studies have shown that most chinooks travel a grand, counter-clockwise circle tour of the North Pacific. Some make the tour once, or even short-cut it, dropping off at the near point to their home stream. Others stay "aboard" the great carousel and make a second, perhaps a third or fourth tour, growing ever heavier. Some mature along the coast, in the inlets. Hence the 20—125-pound variations in weights.

The heaviest chinook I've seen mentioned in print is a 125-pounder, caught in a trap by an Alaskan commercial fisherman in the 1930's. A clipping from the *Vancouver Sun*, dated August 25, 1969, tells of a commercially troll-caught 102-pound chinook taken near Juneau. It was to be mounted and sent to Expo 70 in Japan this year (1970).

Largest sport-caught or rod-and-reel chinook, a 92-pounder, was taken by Terrace, B.C., fishing guide Heinz Wichman, July 19, 1959, from the nearby Skeena River, spin-casting with a Luhr Jensen Krocodile spoon. Wichman was only fourteen at the time. He used a Super Quick reel, a B.C.-assembled brand of glass rod and 25-pound-test line. It took two hours to land and broke the 1920 record of 83 pounds from the Umpqua River, Oregon. It took a long time for the wilder northern area, that obviously breeds heavier salmon and trout, to gain angling recognition.

Outstanding sporting catches by area run to 90 pounds on the Skeena River, 70 pounds on the Kitimat, 82 at Rivers Inlet, 65 at Phillips Arm and Alberni Inlet, over 70 at Campbell River, up to 70 at Comox, up to 50 at Cowichan Bay, Saanich Inlet, Muchalat Inlet, Qualicum Bay, Howe Sound, Sargeant Bay, Pender Harbor, Egmont, Toba Inlet and the Atnarko-Bella Coola River, and up to 35 pounds throughout the winter chinook feeding areas, and most of the runs caught at the Fraser tributary mouths from April to July and as late as August on the South Thompson.

The chinook likely obtained its popular British Columbia name of "spring" because many of them enter the rivers then. The fish has several other locally preferred names the length of the Pacific Coast so it was high time a standard name was chosen when, in 1958, the American Fisheries Society did so. (It actually would be better named the Fisheries Society of the Americas as it now includes many non-United States member scientists.)

Alaskans did and still do call the chinook the king salmon. Washington, Oregon and California anglers know it best as chinook, sometimes call it quinnat and call the immature winter fish "blackmouths" after their black gums. Even New Zealand, where the chinook was introduced successfully decades ago, calls it the quinnat. To further confuse the issue, angling literature, old and recent, calls spring-run Atlantic salmon "springs" or "springers." So, it will be a happier day all round when we all know the fine salmon as the chinook. Some Canadian anglers have asked why we should give in to the U.S. Well, to be fair, they in turn gave in to our popular name for the coho and are attempting, with considerable suc-cess, to popularize coho rather than "silver."

Scientists don't have the problem themselves. Centuries ago they used a standardized Latin terminology, world wide, for all living creatures, and further standardized on the present system suggested just over 100 years ago. Only the layman and the news media, attempting to keep him in touch, still flounder about, if the reader will pardon the pun.

As I review my lifetime fishing log I find I've rather specialized in chinook fishing without intending to. But the very size of British Columbia and the scattered assignments of a fish and game reporter haven't permitted specialization on more than one or two spots. It is the angler who can do so who is the true expert in his own bailiwick. I have managed to look in on most points of chinook interest, however.

There was the amazing first trip to Rivers Inlet in the early 1950's when I boated 15 of 18 tyees hooked in five mornings and two evenings, fish of 28 to 50 pounds, all on artificial lures, all red-fleshed, bright-conditioned. The foregoing 65-pounder from Comox, which the reader may have guessed was my fish, was one of several delightful Comox-Campbell River trips. I've other fond memories of busy or quiet but never tedious hours at chinook spots like the Gold River-mouth at Muchalat Inlet, three different centers on Alberni Inlet, Sooke, Westport in Washington, Saanich Inlet, Active Pass, Discovery Passage, Douglas Channel, Kitimat River, Stuart Island, Hernando Island, Lund, Cockburn Bay, Pender Harbor, Sargeant Bay, Egmont, Porpoise Bay, Britannia Beach and the many other fishy corners of Howe Sound, Ambleside, Point Grey, the Fraser creekmouths from Mission to Spuzzum, and the Lillooet, Thompson and Atnarko rivers.

I've sat for 200 minutes, waiting for a chinook of only 23 pounds to tire enough for me to net it. Just last year (1969) I had two chinooks on 10-pound-test leaders at the same time, a 28-pounder boring due south while a 22-pounder sounded and held on while we weighed anchor and chased the first fish. That little adventure took 75 minutes to sort out.

Sometimes one will fish for days without a nibble, then hook six tyees in one morning. You may nurse a strong fish until the hook wears a hole and drops out of its lip before you can net it. Try to hurry a tyee on super heavy trolling tackle and chances are it'll lose the side off its face before it'll give way. Chinook anglers often have lines cut by passing trollers, sometimes deliberately. In rivers, chinooks turn and ride the current more often than does a coho or steelhead, hence we lose more of them on light tackle. A tyee will deliberately drag your sinker among reef rocks to snap the leader, even as the trout scrubs its nose in river or lake bottom.

Last year a 38-pounder drew my partner and me in our car-top outboard motorboat through the fierce Sechelt Rapids, luckily as it neared high slack, then kept us there 90 minutes, jumping often before we slid its bulk aboard by flashlight and fled ahead of the freshening ebbtide rapids. The next day a 20-pounder took us on a mile-long ride past Egmont, also jumping several times.

I've taken visiting dignitaries to currently hot spots and drawn a blank. Another time, asked to catch a Britannia chinook for a 30-minute television sequence, when they weren't running well at all, I had a 27-pound chinook obligingly take a trolled plug just after sun-up, to show

that technique. Then another waited while I demonstrated herring stripcasting, gulped that herring strip, leaped several times for the camera, waited until the cameraman moved in closer, leapt some more and then came to the net, a 21-pounder.

The chinook salmon is a royal fish—grand in size and spirit, grander still on a platter. He stalks your herring and sniffs it like a fine cigar before he mouths it, and finally, suspiciously tries to gulp it— not like the flashy coho who some days will gobble sinkers.

Whether blowing on your hands to keep warm at Horseshoe Bay's "hole-in-the-wall" on a bitterly damp April day, or trolling under a blistering late July sun at Nahmint Bay in Alberni Inlet, you never know when you'll meet your lifetime top salmon, a chinook of course.

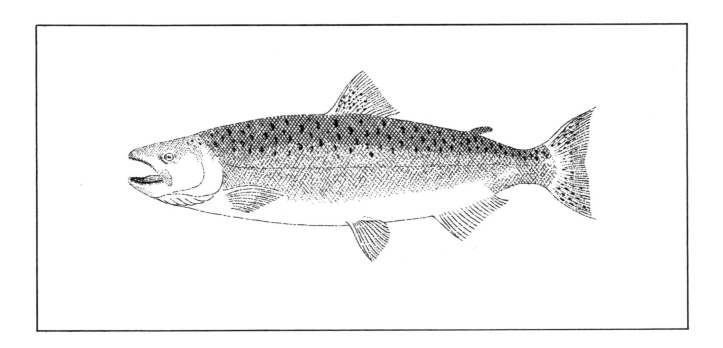

Pete Broomhall

The Steelhead Trout

IN THIS the province of British Columbia, it is not surprising that steelhead are becoming scarcer with each passing season. Rather, it's surprising that steelhead have not yet been totally eliminated from many rivers. And despite attempts to convince the public that the province's sportfishery is in capable hands, it is all too evident that only a major act of conscience could now reverse the trend.

Despite lip service to the contrary, man is worshipping Industry with unabated zeal. And in this province, steelhead are a natural sacrifice. Steelhead use water. So does Industry. Steelhead need clean water. But Industry does not respect purity.

It's a pity that the steelhead's future is so bleak. There simply isn't a superior sportfish in the province—if anywhere. And those who have experienced it know that hooking a steelhead is one of the greatest angling thrills. No matter how steelhead take—whether so gently it's difficult to detect, or with a surface-shattering rush—it is the first few seconds that leave the most indelible impression.

The playing and landing of steelhead are bonuses. For some, the landing is even somewhat anti-climatic. This does not suggest, however, that a hooked steelhead is easily subdued. Far from it. As experienced steelheaders will testify, a fifty percent win-loss average is respectable.

All this is as it should be, for the steelhead is truly a trophy fish. He's as handsome and strong and unpredictable as any angler could wish. Indeed, it would be difficult to imagine anything more attractive than a steelhead fresh in from the sea. His back is dark blue, sometimes almost black. His sides are bright silver, his belly white as snow. The center of the tail fin looks as if it had been lightly streaked with silver paint. The belly fins are translucent. The fresh-run steelhead is moderately spotted mainly above the lateral line.

As the spawning season approaches, the steelhead undergoes a considerable transformation. His sea-silver sides lose their lustre. A pink or reddish band develops from gill plates to tail. The belly becomes greyish. The fins darken. The back often turns several shades lighter—sometimes to a greenish-brown colour. The jaws sharpen, and the spots become more numerous and more apparent.

Steelhead generally spawn during late winter and early spring, though May-June spawning is not uncommon. Unlike Pacific salmon, steelhead may spawn more than once. And although fewer than ten percent are likely to make two spawning migrations, some have been known to spawn three and four times. The young remain in freshwater for about two years before migrating to the sea. The adult steelhead, which average about eight pounds in most rivers, return to the river of their birth during their fourth or fifth year. Rivers renowned for large steelhead—the Squamish, Thompson, Dean, Kispiox, Copper—evidently have more of the five-year-olds than do other watersheds.

The official world record steelhead was taken from the Kispiox River in 1954. It weighed 36 pounds. Appropriately enough, this is one pound less than the official record for rainbow trout. The one-pound difference is appropriate simply because the steelhead *is* a rainbow trout. Essentially, the only difference between the two is that the steelhead visits the sea whereas the rainbow remains loyal to freshwater. The steelhead, then, is a sea-going rainbow trout.

Like the rainbow, the steelhead is a freshwater sportfish. Very few are taken by sea anglers, and, so far, sea catches can be dismissed as accidents. On the other hand, few river catches can be called pure accidents even though steelhead occasionally are suicidally co-operative in freshwater. Perhaps there is even some truth to the observation that the angler who has yet to catch his first steelhead is a beginner while the man who has caught one steelhead is an expert.

It is reasonably certain that anglers would have less reason to fear for the steelhead's future if tycoons and politicians had enough talent to catch them. It is at least true that a relatively small coterie of steelheaders catch the majority of the fish taken. It is also true that, once acquired, the steelhead pox is difficult to shake.

The cure for the affliction, of course, is to go steelhead fishing. But it's a short-term cure, and must frequently be repeated. Happily, B.C. steelheaders can still take the cure year-round. In fact, throughout the steelhead's entire range—California to Alaska—some sea-run rainbows can legitimately be expected during every month of the year. But not in every river or watershed. Even closely neighbouring streams may have widely divergent seasons. For this reason, the steelheader must often be prepared to travel quite extensively. And knowing when the runs peak in various streams is more than somewhat helpful.

The world record steelhead taken from the Kispiox, for example, was encountered during that river's peak month—October. The Squamish River run peaks during April. The Dean is at its best in August. Clearly enough, the steelhead is a sportfish for all seasons. And this is probably why distinctions have been made between the various runs.

To some steelheaders, the distinctions are merely academic: steelhead caught during the winter are winter-runs; those caught during the summer are summer-runs. Accordingly, October Kispiox or Thompson river fish would be fall-runs, and April-caught steelhead would be spring-runs. There are many steelheaders who disagree with this system. They claim that distinctions should be made according to racial characteristics. They point out that winter-run fish beget winter-run fish, and summer

fish beget summer fish. Even biologists have been able to discover differences between winter and summer steelhead.

Understandably, the farther upstream a steelhead journeys, the earlier he is likely to enter freshwater, and the less sexually mature he is likely to be when he leaves the sea. Hence many of the September-November steelhead that frequent many interior rivers—the Thompson, Morice, Babine, Skeena, Kispiox—probably leave the sea during late summer or early fall. Similarly, the shorter a steelhead's journey, the later he is likely to enter freshwater, and the more sexually mature he is likely to be when he leaves the sea. Hence many of the steelhead present in the shorter coastal streams during April and May probably did not leave the sea much beforehand. But calling the former summer-runs and the latter spring-runs might be very misleading.

It is worth noting that the above-mentioned fall- and spring-caught steelhead are both relatively mature when they leave the sea. Their spawn—either roe or milt—extends from about two-thirds to the full extent of the

belly cavity. But true summer-runs are something else. Some of them enter freshwater almost a full year before they are ready to spawn. And they don't always have that far to travel either.

Take the North Shore streams. Regardless of how absurd it sounds, Capilano and Seymour river summer-runs have been taken during the winter—as early as March. Such fish were called *spring-runs*. And they were not easily mistaken. They fought about three times harder than their winter-run brothers; they were also thicker and deeper-bodied than the winter fish.

Back in the days when the Capilano and Seymour had good runs of steelhead, it was fairly common for both the winter and summer breeds to be taken on the same day. Occasionally an exceptionally bright and active late-run winter fish would be mistaken for a summer-run. But a glimpse into the fish's interior would quickly settle matters. Whereas a winter fish would be full of spawn (or already spawned out), the spawn of a summer fish would still be undeveloped. The roe or milt of an eight-pound summer-run might be less than three inches long, and much thinner than a pencil. The summer-run's belly walls would also be very thick and firm. Those who have caught both are usually quick to rank the summer steelhead as the superior of the two.

The abuses heaped on the North Shore streams are particularly offensive when it is realized that the Capilano and Seymour once had good runs of the two distinct races of Steelhead. The overlapping of the runs made steelheading a worthwhile proposition for much of the year. I have caught Capilano steelhead in every month except August. Doubtless many others have taken them in every month. But that's all in the past. And if the past is any indication, other rivers and other runs will continue to be sacrificed. And the more-highly prized summer fish will probably be the first to go.

In many once-good rivers, summer runs are already downright scarce. As recently as May 1969 a friend and I encountered an early run in the Gold River on Vancouver Island. But there weren't many, and I suspect the Gold's summer-run steelhead will rapidly decline—if not altogether disappear. There's a pulp operation there now, and angling pressure is also increasing. The Morice River—tributary to the Skeena—is likewise fated. For that matter, so is the Thompson. In short, it's happening throughout the entire province.

With each succeeding year, the situation deteriorates a little bit more. And with each succeeding year, steelheaders are forced to search a little farther afield. It's no wonder that more and more B.C. steelheaders are turning to Washington and Oregon states—particularly for summer steelhead. Those states are at least taking measures to save their steelhead.

When it comes to catching steelhead, however, there's little difference between the two countries. U.S. anglers seem to be ahead in certain particulars, B.C. anglers in others. In time, B.C. steelheaders will probably adopt the smaller rods and multiplier reels so very much in vogue among U.S. steelheaders. Several of my steelheader friends have already purchased the Ambassador reel. And they're using it with increasing frequency, particularly on big rivers such as the Gold, Campbell, Squamish, or Thompson. But, unlike U.S. steelheaders, my friends remain loyal to longish rods—ten to eleven feet. The persisting claim is that the long rod makes for easier float-fishing. In time, however, the long float rod will likely go the way of the long fly rod. And, significantly, it was U.S. flyfishers who occasioned the fly-rod revolution.

If any B.C. inspired steelhead fishing revolution ever occurs in the states, it will most likely be float-fishing. For some inexplicable reason, float-fishing is still virtually unknown to U.S. steelheaders. At least not to the point where they are doing it. Float-fishing has been practiced in B.C. for many years, and many U.S. visitors have seen it done on various rivers throughout the province. But they haven't yet taken the idea across the border. Even so, the idea has crossed the border—to several Washington and Oregon state rivers. And it proved as effective as we'd expect. But it was done by B.C. steelheaders who would be happy if U.S. steelheaders continue to regard float-fishing as a quaint exercise.

No matter if it's drifting, spinning, or float-fishing, a day's observation on almost any popular steelhead stream is enough to give a B.C. hopeful a few hints about both tackle and techniques. Not so with flyfishing. Although it is true that the art is at long last gaining a respectable following—in part due to tackle improvements spearheaded by U.S. manufacturers—flyfishers are not yet an everyday sight on steelhead streams. And although flyfishing is still not recognized as an efficient means of catching steelhead, it does deserve mention. It is probably the most satisfying way to catch sea-run rainbows.

The very acme of steelheading is to catch a summer-run fish on the dry fly. Even those citizens who are barely warm would get more than a little excited about an eight-pound summer-run rising to a floating fly. Nor should dry-fly fishing for summer-runs be dismissed as a labour of love. According to many veterans of the technique, summer-runs will often refuse everything *except* the dry fly.

The refusal to accept baits and lures is not confined to summer-run steelhead. At times, the closed-mouthedness of steelhead becomes a source of extreme frustration. Particularly when one can watch them as they refuse all baits and lures. Sometimes, too, steelhead resolutely refuse one angler's offerings while willingly accepting others. Many anglers, it seems, are destined to be jinxed.

I have known several such men. One is especially memorable. He was rather tweedy. Rather natty. A mustached

43

pipe smoker. But jolly keen. In spite of rain or snow, he religiously visited the same popular steelhead pool Sunday after Sunday. He used the same float-fishing tackle as the regulars used—right down to the number and size of split shot. He cast where they cast. And to all appearances, he did all the right things. But though others caught fish, he didn't.

Like the others, he would stand with his feet poking through the bottom rungs of the guardrail of a bridge that conveniently crossed directly over the pool. This perch provided one main advantage: when the river was running clear, he could look directly into the pool. And he soon was spotting steelhead as readily as the regulars. He even learned how to follow the baits as they drifted down the current. Occasionally he would see a fish move and take a bait. But it was never his bait. When his bait drifted directly toward a fish, the fish would invariably move aside.

And then one sunny day in late winter, there was a change. He was quietly watching his bait as it drifted serenely through the depths when a steelhead calmly took it. He saw the white mouth open and close. It was several seconds before he realized that it was his bait that had disappeared. Then he got excited.

First he leaned a little too far over the bridge rail—the better to see the fish—and a tackle box fell out of his

jacket's upper pocket and into the river. Then he straightened up, and in the process kicked his bait tin into the river. He then struck too hard, which annoyed the steelhead considerably. At this point, he lost his remaining composure. He clamped down on both his reel and his pipe. He bit clean through the pipe stem. The Brier and the steelhead hit the surface at the same moment. He saw neither again.

Few would-be steelheaders are stoic enough to continue their steelhead quest in the face of impossible odds. Every now and then they must hook a fish. Otherwise, the disillusionment becomes unbearable. A friend and I once met a singularly sad beginner. Like so many tourists, he had been hooked on tourist-promotion bait. He had driven from Twin Falls, Idaho, fully convinced there was no way he could avoid catching many steelhead in British Columbia.

He was moderately experienced in the ways of lesser fish such as bass, and he carried respectable tackle. We met him when he impulsively stopped at our campsite one sunny September afternoon. He just wanted to know how we'd been doing. When he told us that he hadn't even hooked one fish during his two weeks of trying, that the more successful hotel guests had been ribbing him unmercifully for several days, and that he had to leave in two days, we decided to invite him to join us for a day. We reasoned that he couldn't do worse.

He was at our campsite ahead of the appointed hour. Soon we were on our favourite spot, the Meadow Pool, and soon we had made the necessary adjustments to his tackle. My friend and I had fished the pool many times. We were fairly certain we knew the best holding water. Accordingly, we directed his casting and retrieving with considerable care. We even made him stand on a big slope-sided boulder that just happened to be the best station from which to drift a lure. He even tried to climb off the rock at one point, complaining that it was a mighty uncomfortable rock to perch on, but our glares held him at bay.

His first cast splashed down about thirty feet too far downstream. His second cast was too far upstream, and not far enough across. We patiently coaxed him on saying that if he didn't soon get the spinner in the right place, we'd chuck him in the river. After he'd cast to the right spot a couple of times, we told him when to stop reeling, when to let the lure sink. We were getting somewhat fidgety by this time. The morning sun was almost on the water. And in that particular spot we had hooked fish only during the pre- and post-sun hours.

Finally everything clicked. The spinner touched down

in the right spot. He retrieved till it was just upstream of the small hole, and he started his drift right on target. Because he was new to steelheading, our American guest could be forgiven for not knowing that a steelhead had gently stopped the drifting lure. My friend and I were both watching the rod tip. When it assumed a tell-tale slight bend, we both shouted "strike." The American nearly fell off the rock, but somehow his rock-top balancing act managed to jar the fish.

The battle was one of those fairly standard affairs—punctuated with several speedy sprints and leaps. Our guest became increasingly nervous as the fish tired. He wanted to know where the net was. We told him that we never carried such truck, and that we generally put our

fish back anyway—if they didn't get free on their own. He then wanted to know what we did if someone decided to keep a fish. "We stone 'em," we answered, and to illustrate, we picked up a couple of fist-sized rocks. At this he became visibly distressed. Somehow he managed to trust us enough. When the steelhead's belly touched the shore, we tailed him high and dry. We shook hands all around, weighed the fish, and took several snapshots.

The steelhead, a male, was a wonderfully bright eighteen-pounder. For all I know, our American guest might never catch another. But from his face I knew that even if he never again fished for sea-run rainbows, he would always remember the day when he and a silver steelhead met.

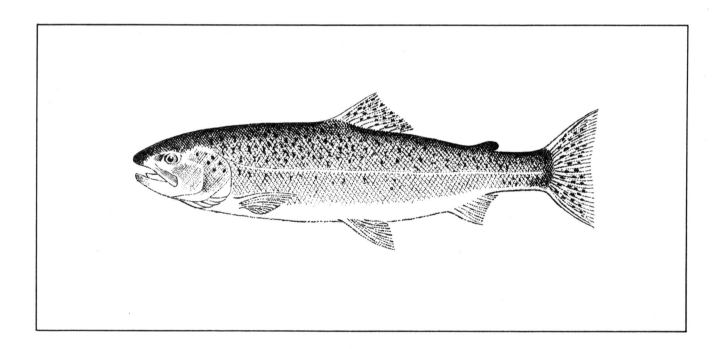

Howard Paish

The Eastern Brook Trout

MENTION the word "trout" anywhere in the eastern part of this continent and right away you will be talking about a char—the speckled char, *Salvinelus Fontinalis*—dubbed a trout by the first settlers and revered by generations of Americans as *the* trout, a game fish famous before the great land move west and the unlocking of the Pacific watersheds introduced Americans to the cutthroat and the rainbow.

The Beaverkill, the Hudson, and the trout streams of the Catskills, the Adirondacks, and the Smokey Mountains were already enshrined in the angling lore of a continent when the Umpqua, the Kispiox, the Sustut, and the Dean were still unnamed rivers in an undiscovered land.

The speckled char, or the eastern brook trout as we shall call him from this point on, is a pretty fish. He is shaped like a trout, though generally in this province, probably because of the water we have put him into, he tends to be rather on the deep side and not as streamlined as the rainbow or the cutthroat. The basic colour is dark olive green on the back, tapering to a lighter olive on the sides, and almost white underneath, with worm-like markings or vermiculations on the back and dorsal fin. On the sides he is covered with small greenish spots, some with red centres and some bordered with blue. The tail and lower fins are pinkish and there is a distinct white streak around the front of the lower fins. The spawning colouration of the eastern brook trout, particularly the male, gives him a really gaudy appearance. The lighter olive of his sides turns almost to a yellow, the fins appear redder and a reddish streak appears along the lower flank. In addition the spots appear brighter, probably because of the change in the background.

Brook trout have been recorded up to three feet in length and the heaviest recorded is a 14½-pounder from the Nipigon River in Ontario. As far as I have been able to discover, the best fish recorded in British Columbia was a nine-pounder from Loon Lake near Nelson, caught by the daughter of a well-known west Kootenay sportsman, the late Mickey McEwan. Fish of five pounds are not uncommon in a number of eastern brook trout lakes in this province.

In the east, particularly in some of the well-known, relatively unexploited rivers in Quebec, and in Manitoba's God's River, the eastern runs up to seven pounds. There have been no records of fish anywhere near that weight in streams in British Columbia. I have yet to hear of one bigger than two pounds. For the most part, where the eastern brook trout has adapted to streams out here, it has quickly overpopulated them and, of course, the population tapers off at a pretty small fish, in the six- to nine-inch class.

Under normal conditions eastern brook trout spawn in the fall and, as with other trout and salmon, the eggs are deposited in gravelly streams, with fry emerging the following March.

Few of the eastern brook that are found in lakes in British Columbia have a chance to spawn. For the most part they are found in lakes with poor spawning oppor-

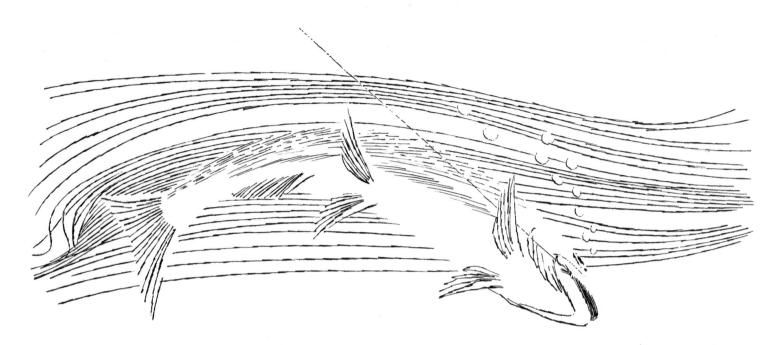

tunities. It is not an uncommon sight to find the fish in November trying to find a shoreline spawning area, but the eggs are usually reabsorbed into the fish's system.

The eastern brook trout is mainly an insect feeder, and his food preferences are similar to the rainbow. He has generally been introduced into those British Columbia lakes that have an abundant food supply, usually a heavy shrimp population. The larger eastern brook trout are predacious to some extent, but insects, rather than small fish, make up the major part of their diet. In part, this may be due to the somewhat artificial conditions under which they are generally found in British Columbia. We don't know the answers, because little serious study has been made of the eastern brook trout as he actually exists here.

When you read in some of the classic trout texts written about the eastern brook trout of the east—about his habits and certainly about the kind of waters in which he is found, and methods of angling for him—you ask yourself if you are reading about the same fish as the eastern brook trout we have here in British Columbia.

British Columbia anglers are spoiled. Not just contemptuous of anything except the salmonids (salmon and trout and char), we're even fussy about which of those we are ready to class a real game fish.

Our fresh water fisherman, for the most part, is hooked on the Kamloops trout and his classy sea-run counterpart, the steelhead. True, as this book illustrates, keen anglers are beginning to realize the tremendous challenge of the cutthroat, particularly the sea-runs. A few anglers are realizing the potential of that dry-fly delight, the Arctic grayling. The kokanee is no longer simply a forage fish for rainbows that sometimes reaches a catchable

size of 12 to 14 inches. He is now a sports fish in his own right—understandable when it's possible now to catch him upwards of eight pounds. The angler who is prepared to toss away the wire line, two-pound weights, and fish for the lake trout on light tackle, even fly tackle with streamer flies, is realizing the potential of the lake trout. But by and large the anglers who fish B.C. waters, residents and visitors alike, are completely overawed by the rainbow. The continent's classic trout, the eastern brook trout, is usually a chunk of meat yarded up through a hole in the ice at the end of a piece of cuttyhunk, with a marshmallow or kernel of corn for bait.

At this point I am not knocking ice fishing as such. What I am suggesting, however, is that we are certainly missing something by not going after the eastern brook trout by the more conventional angling methods that we reserve for the rainbow.

Lest my motives be misunderstood here, I should stress that fly-fishing for rainbow is very near the top of my list of outdoor pleasures. But I am enough of a realist to realize that we have vast bodies of water in British Columbia that will never produce quality rainbows, and I happen to think that we will shortchange ourselves in the long run by placing so much emphasis on the rainbow (even to the point, a few years ago, of tolerating the release into B.C. waters of domestic rainbow stock).

I say this for two good reasons. First, there is no question that by recognizing the diversity of angling pleasure offered by the pursuit of a different quarry we can add to the sum total of fishing pleasure. I think back to the angling pleasure of my boyhood, when, while I had plenty of opportunities to fish for brown trout, and did, I enjoyed, every bit as much, fishing seriously for what we

48

here disdainfully cast to one side as trash fish. In many parts of the world the carp is a trophy fish, and the close relatives of our chub, squawfish and sucker provide the bulk of the sport of European anglers. As I said earlier, we are spoiled, and we have our salmonid fixation, but we are also lucky, because within the salmon group alone we have diversity. Forgetting for the moment the imperatives that a growing population and a greater demand for angling opportunity will place upon our sports fisheries—even if we could keep the almost unlimited angling opportunities we have had until quite recently—there is merit in being able to enjoy the diversity that a range of species can give us.

Perhaps far more important in the long run, however, as we are discovering almost daily, is the steady loss of what we have traditionally considered natural fish habitat. And, where we don't lose habitat outright, increasing pressures are being placed upon that habitat by an ever growing army of anglers and other outdoor recreationists. It would be wonderful if we could turn the clock back and pretend that the impact of technology would pass us by. Too many of us have done that for too long, and we start to cry about the loss of our favourite stream long after any real chance of saving it has passed us by. We have to realize, of course, that we too can apply to our advantage the tools of technology—systems analysis, critical path thinking, and all the things that are having such an impact on our environment, and very directly on our sports fishing. The kind of technology that can talk seriously about genetic engineering and can put men on the moon can help us bring so many of our seemingly unproductive water bodies into use as fish producers, if we consider the effort worthwhile—and if we are prepared to foot the bill.

The eastern brook trout and the European brown trout have been the two members of the salmonid group that have been successfully introduced into British Columbia waters. The brown trout introduction has had limited success. The fish has succeeded in the Cowichan River but not elsewhere.

The eastern brook trout was first introduced into B.C. in 1908 at the time when most provinces and states were experimenting widely with the introduction of exotics. The B.C. introduction was made from eggs obtained in Quebec, and little record appears to have been kept of the exact location of the first, and soon-following releases in B.C. It is known, however, that the fish were introduced on Vancouver Island, some lakes in the Lower Mainland and across the southern part of the province. They are still present on Vancouver Island, in the upper

reaches of tributaries of the Cowichan River, and while no up-to-date records of catches have been made, they were reported to have been present in Spectacle Lake and Somenos Lake on Vancouver Island during the 1950's. The eastern brook trout has not survived in the Lower Mainland, but has caught on in the Interior, in the Kootenays, and as far north as Prince George. But more on his present distribution later.

As more has been learned about the life habits of the eastern brook trout and his suitability for distribution in British Columbia, rather important points have been found in his favour. First, he can tolerate far higher summer water temperatures than the rainbow and far lower water temperatures in the winter. But perhaps most important of all for our ice-covered interior lakes, he can tolerate a far lower oxygen level than the rainbow. In addition the fish seems to be far more active in winter, which is particularly important to the ice fisherman.

Because of these particular water characteristics, because the Kamloops is for the most part so well adapted to streams, and, because most of our recent fish culture programs have been aimed at lakes, the eastern brookie has been introduced extensively into fairly shallow, sluggish lakes in the southern and central parts of the province. As a result he has a reputation for being a somewhat sluggish fighter. A far cry indeed from his habits on some of the wild brawling streams where he is found in his native habitat. God's River in Manitoba, for example, and the eastern streams of the areas referred to earlier are very different from the pothole-type lake that we look to as traditional eastern brook trout water in this province.

When we get down to serious fisheries management in this province, and find it necessary to make introductions in presently unproductive streams, as we inevitably will, the eastern brook trout may well be the fish that will adapt to our Arctic watershed rivers—which do not suit the rainbow. The stream-flow characteristics, indeed the whole countryside around some of our northern streams, is somewhat similar to the native streams of the eastern brook trout. Of course, there may well be totally different soil conditions and stream characteristics that would make these streams unsuitable for his introduction. However, I have a strong hunch that when we do get down to serious fisheries management and start looking towards stream habitat improvement and major introductions on a far wider scale that we are able to at present, we will be thinking very seriously about the eastern brook trout for some of our northern rivers.

It is very difficult to determine just how much of a contribution the eastern brook trout makes to our provincial fisheries at the present time. There is no question that it makes up a large component of the ice-fishing catch, and there is no question that one of the management objectives in this province for the eastern brook trout is to cater to this type of fishing. This, of course, will make the rainbow trout fisherman happy because it will take the pressure off his beloved rainbow, and at the same time provide a completely different type of angling for those who want it.

The anglers who have taken the trouble to learn the ways of the eastern brook trout seem to be a rather close lot, rather like the coastal cutthroat fishermen, who enjoy their sport and don't spread the fact too widely.

When I look back over many enjoyable fishing experiences in this province, some that really stand out have been with the eastern brook. A 1956 Easter holiday trip in the little Slocan Valley near Slocan in the West Kootenays was my first real introduction to the eastern brook trout. I snowshoed into some beaver ponds (in those days snowshoeing eight or 10 miles came pretty easily), and I was to learn—once I got around to reading Ray Bergman and Robert Travers a number of years later—that I had enjoyed a traditional and almost classical opening day on brook trout. The creek was open, the willows just beginning to sprout, the first few ducks were back and almost every cast into the oily green water of the pond produced a fish. I don't know how many I caught and released that day, but I know I took home a pretty good feed of brook trout from 12 to 14 inches. I went back often over the next three years. My last visit came late in the summer about 12 years later. A major forestry road had led to the blasting of the beaver dams. Hordes of summer picnickers had probably taken care of the few fish that remained in the stream. Perhaps I didn't try quite hard enough, but I know I deserted the eastern brook trout, and ended up having a delightful evening of rainbow fishing on the Slocan River. However that's another story.

My next serious encounter with eastern brook trout was at a little unamed lake in the Findlay Creek watershed in the East Kootenays in late October. A doldrum day for big-game hunting, but worth poking around taking a look at the sloughs to see if any moose tracks might point to where I should be sitting at dusk. I knew that eastern brook trout had been planted in a few of the small lakes around Canal Flats, but since I moved up there at the start of the hunting season, I had been too interested in hunting to worry too much about the fishing. The sound, and then the size of the splashes, as I walked a couple of hundred yards from my jeep to a little pot-

hole of no more than an acre, soon had me scurrying back to see what fishing tackle I could put together. It wasn't much, a spinning outfit and rather poor selection of lures. Those fish were hungry, and all that I had learned about the eastern brook trout being primarily an insect feeder went right out the window. I ended up with eight or nine eastern brooks, the smallest of which was a pound and a half—the biggest close to three pounds. Before I could get back to the lake to fish it again it had frozen over, and by the time the back roads were open again it was late May.

This time I was prepared to do the job in style. I had a small rubber raft and fly tackle. The water was gin clear and small trout were rippling the surface everywhere, feeding on something that I am sure could only be imitated by the tiniest midge on a number 22 hook. I tried for them for several hours. I caught one on the smallest midge, size 18 I think, that I could dig out of my box. When the angle of the sun moved to a point where I could see deeper into the water, a movement in the weeds caught my attention. I hadn't a fast-sinking line with me so a couple of shot on the leader did the trick. A shrimp fly over the weed beds produced a strike first cast, and I was in business again. I caught half a dozen fish between two and three pounds, all in prime condition. I discovered on several subsequent visits, however, that in a body of water that size, I had probably caught most of the big fish on that trip and the one the previous fall, because try as I might I rarely caught more than one of the big fish per trip. However, the eight- or nine-inchers that were coming along became more catchable and I taxed my eyes to tie smaller flies. The following winter, as sometimes happens with eastern brook lakes in this province, the lake winter killed. I haven't been back.

I had become hooked on the eastern brook trout again, and soon found that a couple of Kimberley anglers I knew well, Carl Galicano and Ted McVicker, took the eastern brook trout pretty seriously. They told me that several lakes in the Invermere area—Enid, Wilmer and Dorothy—were good in May and June before the water became too warm. These lakes were within an hour's drive from my home, and while frustration was sometimes the order of the day, it was sometimes rewarded with near limit catches of fish to nearly four pounds just at dusk. Other times they would be biting all day. A rather intriguing part about this apprenticeship at eastern brook trout fishing was the fact that all the lakes we fished were strictly for fly fishing, for the simple reason that by June they were filled with weeds. That, I suspect, is one reason why eastern brook trout haven't become too popular in

this province; their habitat doesn't lend itself to trolling.

My most recent trip for eastern brook was undertaken deliberately to refresh a few memories for this chapter. In three years I had fished for them just once—on a busy late May weekend—and had a dozen brook trout between one and two pounds on one of the small lakes right by the Caribou Highway, a few miles south of Clinton. I had spent the day trying for rainbows under conditions that were just about impossible. I dropped to a lower elevation and had a ball while the other frustrated rainbow anglers were heading home skunked. That day was one of the days I have been able to catch them on spinning tackle, though I suspect that they go well for lures if you can find a body of water clear enough in which to use them.

Since then I had watched with interest the development of the ice fishery on the lakes around Williams Lake, and while I hadn't tried it, I knew that if the fish were there in mid-winter they had to be there the rest of the year. A chat with a local pro put me in business and the result surprised me. In four days I don't think I saw a fish surface feed, yet at almost any time of the day on a fast-sinking line I could take fish. It took me three or four hours to realize that the sparsely dressed shrimp fly that I had found effective in the Kootenays didn't work around Williams Lake and that conservation officer-angler Pat Mulligan's advice to use something bright paid off. Light penetration into the water was three feet at the most, and although the fish were full of shrimp, visibility of the fly seemed to be most important.

It has been my experience that any wet fly method that works for rainbows, works for brook trout. If big eastern brooks go on surface feeding sprees I have yet to see them, although I am quite sure that sometime or another they must. I have seen the smaller fish surface feeding. They are invariably feeding on really minute flies that are very difficult to match. A fast sinking line and a fairly jerky retrieve, bringing in only a few inches of line at a time over the weed beds, seems to work best. Watch shrimp swim sometimes and you'll realize why. I found that a sparsely-tied shrimp imitation on a number eight or 10 hook was the best bet in the East Kootenays, and that these flies worked well on Co-op Lake near Burns Lake and Vivian near Prince George. At Dugan, Skulow, and other water around Williams Lake, silver- and gold-bodied flies, with dull-brown wings and hackles seem to be the best producers. The most important point I think, is a sinking line, with the fly right down in the weeds.

When conditions permit spin fishing for brook trout, precisely the same lures that take rainbows will work. I have tried it seldom since I'm not too keen on spinning, but people who have tried spinning outfits right after ice-out, and before the weeds build seem to do well. I have never trolled hardware for brook trout (because I don't like trolling hardware for anything), but I suspect that under most summer conditions, weeds would create real problems for the troller.

Naturally, the eastern brook trout is a bait-dunker's delight. Worms, corn, chunks of cheese—all the baits that the ice fisherman uses, produce fish in the summer. The kids love him.

No discussion of eastern brook trout in B.C. would be complete without a mention of ice fishing, because this is where the eastern brook trout appears to have provided the best fishery in this province. As I have already suggested, perhaps if we stop to figure out why he provides such a good winter fishery, we may use that as a clue to putting him into the kind of water in this province where he could also be a better prospect for the summer angler.

I know just how some of the other anglers who have contributed to this book react to ice fishing. I react precisely the same way when we are talking about catching rainbow trout in lakes that can provide super summer fishing. However, I don't think it is fair to try to compare ice fishing in waters that are managed specifically for that purpose with any other form of angling. That it often lends itself to a meat hunting exercise, that the fish can be vulnerable, and that all kinds of regulations can be violated is equally true of some summer fisheries. The people who are doing the fishing, not the angling method, create the problem here. Compared with most conventional angling, ice fishing is easy. It is fun sometimes, however, to stretch out on the ice, naturally with something warm underneath, to see just what is going on under the surface; and there is quite a thrill, if you are prepared to accept it as a new fishing experience, to watch the fish nosing around the bait. The experience is a little more like hunting than most forms of angling. Perhaps, as much as anything, it is a good excuse to be outdoors in the winter, and it is rather interesting to note that the strongest critics of ice-fishing rarely come from the areas that enjoy a four- or five-month freeze-up.

How does a brook trout compare with our other game fish, particularly the rainbow?

On the table he is every bit as good and generally superior to the rainbow in the spring and winter months.

Of course, as food, neither of them are in the same league as the kokanee in my book. Because of the kind of water he is usually found in, the brookie's flesh tends to be on the soft side during July and August. A few that I have taken from small, cooler streams during the summer have been good.

As a fighter, he won't engage in the spectacular leaps of the rainbow. He is a strong but deep running fish, more like the brown trout and cutthroat than the rainbow. Under most conditions, he is a more cautious fish than the rainbow. His strike is a very delicate pluck and particularly in summer fly fishing, he is a harder fish to catch, cautious of heavy leaders, and because he lives in lakes where the living is pretty good, he is fussier about his feeding.

I am sure that as time goes on, and as we tend to turn to more intensive fisheries programs in this province, the eastern brook trout, unquestionably our most successful imported fish, will become more and more important to us.

It is becoming patently obvious that although we really know very little about the recreation potential of the north country, and although we often write the fishery off rather simply—because we think of it in light of our experience in the south—the country in the Arctic watershed of B.C. is going to be of immense importance for outdoor recreation in the future. It may well be that 20 years from now we will be enjoying eastern brook trout fishing in waters under precisely the same conditions that settlers in the east enjoyed their "trout" long before the rainbow was even heard of.

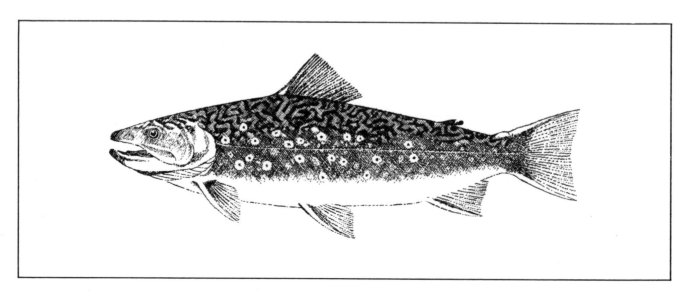

Dave Hurn

The Brown Trout

DESPITE the fact that comparatively few British Columbians have ever fished for brown trout, the brown deserves to be ranked among this province's principle game fish. And there's a good reason why brown trout have attracted so little angling attention: they are scarce. Hopefully, they will one day be more numerous—and better appreciated. And it could well be that the growing demand for quality sport fishing will be a deciding factor.

Brown trout are not native to British Columbia. B.C. anglers often call the brown an *exotic* fish. But names won't hurt him, or render him any less desirable, or handsome. Browns are the province's most colourful trout. They generally are a rich golden brown colour. They wear large, dark spots, some of which have bluish haloes. The spots near the lateral line are often tinged with orange; the spots on the lower flanks are often red-tinged. The tail fin is almost square, and the dark belly fins are often edged with white.

At present, brown trout are found in only three streams in the province—the Cowichan, Little Qualicum, and Kettle. A fourth stream, the Similkameen, may be stocked in the near future. Both the Cowichan and Little Qualicum received their plantings of brown trout during the early 1930's. The Kettle was planted in 1957. In time, the Kettle may become a good brown trout stream; it is still too early to judge.

The three streams which already have browns, and the Similkameen which doesn't, share an essential characteristic: each has a stretch, or stretches, of water that appear to be suitable brown trout habitat. The Cowichan and Little Qualicum are on Vancouver Island's east coast. The Kettle and Similkameen are in the province's southern interior. The Similkameen is the most familiar simply because it is paralleled by a highway from its source in Manning Park to where it runs into the Okanagan River at Oroville in the U.S. The Similkameen has been extensively studied, and the two brown trout experts who were consulted rated much of the river eminently suitable for browns.

The Similkameen's upper reaches are basically stable. At Similkameen Falls, the river is markedly steeper. Vertical drops are common, and only large boulders and bedrock are able to resist the river's violent pounding. Near Princeton, the gradient lessens. Riffles, runs, and occasional deep pools appear. Here the river is less stable than in the upper reaches. The riverbed consists of everything from washed boulders to fine gravel.

The most promising portion of the Similkameen begins near Hedley and extends to the U.S. border. At Hedley, the river assumes a pool-riffle nature. Long pools six and seven feet deep are not uncommon. In places, the current is sufficiently strong to create white water or standing waves. At Keremeos, the river flows across a flood plain. The river course is fairly fixed, and the gradient is slight. The pools and riffles of this section provide good cover and ideal spawning and feeding opportunities. Below the border, the Similkameen begins to look and behave like an estuary. It becomes increasingly silty and meandering, and has fewer and fewer riffles.

I have good reason to think that the Similkameen's middle section—from Hedley to the U.S. border—could provide good brown trout fishing. In the first place, it closely approximates that part of the Cowichan which already provides what I consider to be the most fascinating river fishery in this province. I have had the opportunity to study the Cowichan River in detail, and, in my estimation, it is the province's best brown trout water. And it is presently the only B.C. stream that consistently produces significant catches of brown trout. The Cowichan's browns are also the province's largest. I have heard of eight-pounders from the Kettle River at Midway, but have neither seen them nor yet had the opportunity to fish for them. But I know that Cowichan browns often attain a weight of 10 pounds.

Fortunately, the Cowichan is one of the few B.C. rivers for which comprehensive records have been maintained. And the records date back half a century. Up until, and through most of the 1930's, the Cowichan was literally world-renowned. News on Cowichan River fishing was often more easily obtained in London, New York, or San Francisco than in Vancouver. It was a tremendous fishery, and it was a native trout fishery. It lasted until the mid '30's when the process of stripping the watershed's timber gained momentum.

The results of deforestation were dramatic. Banks were overrun, new channels were cut, and the bottoms were scoured. The whole ecology of the stream was upset. It was into this chaotic situation that the brown trout were introduced. Plantings were made from 1932 through 1936. The exotics did not simply take over from the native trout; they established themselves gradually as the river made a slow comeback with the growth of new ground cover.

In the mid-1950's something unusual occurred. The establishment of a pulp mill actually helped in the recovery of a river, instead of contributing to its downfall. Because the mill at Crofton needed a steady supply of water, a control weir was constructed at the outlet of Cowichan Lake. Happily for fish and fishermen, it was decided to allow the water simply to follow its natural course, and to be removed as required near Duncan. Had the water been taken right at the weir, there would be neither brown trout, rainbow, nor salmon in the Cowichan today.

Construction of this control weir largely stabilized the river flow. During the spring freshet, when roaring floods might normally occur, much water is arrested. The surplus water is released later as the stream flow diminishes. This has helped all species in the Cowichan. Meanwhile, the forests are also coming back, and this will further stabilize the water flow.

The Cowichan may be divided into three distinct zones: the upper, middle, and lower reaches. I doubt that the lower reaches holds many of its own brown trout. Occasionally browns are there, but I believe they have merely dropped back into the Cowichan from the lower reaches of Somenos Creek, a tributary that has its own browns. It is the Cowichan's middle and upper sections which offer the good trout fishing. And it is possible to take both rainbows and browns from either section.

The upper section, some 12 miles in all, stretches downstream from the outlet of Cowichan Lake to Skutz Falls. Here the river has a low gradient. It winds a tortuous course which marks the path it cut through the restraining valley. The series of pools and riffles resembles the U.S. border-to-Keremeos portion of the Similkameen River. The long pools and runs are evenly separated by beautiful, dancing riffles. The runs are moderately deep—usually seven or eight feet. The pools occur at the bends in the river, and are deep—10 to 20 feet. The riverbanks are quite high and well treed, and the river is navigable in either direction. It is best, particularly when trying for browns, to fish from a boat downstream of the well-known Harris Hole.

The middle portion of the river stretches from below Skutz Falls to well above Somenos Creek. This section is known as the Riverbottom. It resembles the Keremeos-Hedley section of the Similkameen. Big trees sweep the river. The river's course and bottom show signs of periodic but moderate changes. The river is quite wide, not very deep, and well gravelled. For the most part, the Riverbottom can be fished from shore, or by wading.

Downstream of the Riverbottom, the Cowichan starts to cut its way through tilted bedrock. This hard-to-fish canyon extends to where the river breaks out onto the estuarial plain at Duncan. (A rather short but truly fantastic canyon occurs below Skutz Falls. It is almost totally unapproachable. You can't climb down into it; you can't wade into it from either end. A few intrepid rivermen have floated into it during periods of medium high water, but it's an extremely tricky proposition.)

Both the upper and middle sections of the Cowichan hold good populations of brown trout. At certain times there are also good numbers of rainbow. The rainbow drop down from the lake in late autumn, distributing themselves on or adjacent to their spawning grounds. Cowichan rainbows recover quickly from their February-

March spawning. Many of the repairing kelts distribute themselves well down the middle section of the river. They then provide excellent sport. But they also detract from the brown trout. For this reason, I favor the upper portion of the river, above Skutz Falls.

More browns are taken from the Cowichan during the spring than at any other season. And during the freshet, spin and bait casters have the decided advantage over fly fishermen. The browns are clean and hard, though not yet in peak condition. And because they have had little opportunity to feed seriously since they spawned in October, they are eager.

Nobody knows exactly where Cowichan brown trout spawn. Furthermore, I don't know of anyone who has managed to locate the young browns. I do know where to find browns just before they spawn. And I do know that they make a big migrational shift during late September and early October. I learned this much by drifting the river above Skutz Falls.

On an average day in July, August, or early September, I would spot 25 to 40 browns in the Broadway Run, a

beautiful piece of water ranging from four to seven feet deep over its one-third mile length. By October the run would be barren.

The very deep Breakfast Hole, less than a half mile upstream, would have no more than 10 to 15 browns on an average summer day. But in October, when the Broadway run was empty, there would be as many as 80 browns in the Breakfast Hole. And some of them were obviously 10-pounders.

Before World War II, browns were known to spawn in Hatchery Creek, which runs through the village of Lake Cowichan. The creek no longer has year-round flow. And since the Cowichan still has brown trout, they must be spawning elsewhere.

It is known that Cowichan browns make two distinct migrations per year: the pre-spawning gathering just described, and the post-spawning redistribution. The redistribution occurs during the spring freshet. As the water warms, the browns consolidate their positions. One of the notable characteristics of the brown is his habit of protecting the territory he claims. Browns become territorially fixed during May or early June, depending on water temperature and flow. Conditions can change dramatically within one week. I rather appreciate the brown's territorial dependability. It means that I can repeatedly visit a particular piece of water, and try for the same fish each time. And because browns tend to segregate by size, I can also choose to fish the water that holds the size of brown trout I prefer. If I encounter a big brown, I know there is an excellent chance that there are other big browns nearby.

Cowichan River brown trout fly-fishing is usually at its best from about mid-May until mid-July. During this period, water temperatures range from 55 to 65 degrees. When the water reaches 70 degrees or higher, as it often does, browns become uncomfortable, and dour.

Browns are equally sensitive to light. During the bright daylight hours, they tend to hold up in the deeper protected pools. As the light fades, they move to the riffles and open runs. Undoubtedly it is best to fish for them at the heels and toes of riffles. Some browns take up relatively permanent residence in whitewater runs. During the low water periods of summer, many such runs will be no wider than 20 feet, but the cresting waves, or *roostertails*, may stand three feet high. The light-sensitive brown finds both cover and feed beneath the turbulence. Because much of the surface light is reflected by the turbulent white water, relatively little light reaches the bottom. The browns quietly lie there, unseen and secure.

Robinson's Reach is one of the finer whitewater runs.

The roostertail there is eight to 10 feet wide, and the waves stand two feet high. There is no sense using a dainty No. 14 or 16 fly in Robinson's Run; it has to be the whole chicken. The browns take the big flies right in the surface turbulence.

In quieter runs and pools, browns are often audible feeders. As the light fades, and as the browns begin to take their insect dinners from the surface, the *plop*, *plop*, *plop* sound begins. Some experienced fly fishermen can tell the fish's size by the sound. Sometimes the sounds of feeding continue most of the night.

Among the Cowichan River oldtimers are a group from Victoria who wouldn't think of fishing for the browns during the daylight hours. They often make their appearance on Friday evenings. They merely sit reading books or listening to the radio until 10 o'clock news. *Then* they go fishing. They know the water; they know the rocks; and they know the back-cast hazards. They muck about in the dark with great Dusty Millers and White Moths, and they catch great tackle-straining browns.

Some runs seem to hold browns both day and night. I call one such spot the Bias Run. It's a short distance above the Cabin Pool. On several occasions I have seen

fishermen leave the Bias Run empty-handed after fishing it fairly thoroughly. They were often convinced the run was fishless. Yet there would invariably be 20 to 30 browns lying on the light-colored sand. They were almost invisible. To spot them, one had to know exactly where and how to look.

In fishing wet or dry flies for browns, I don't recall hooking fish until the sweep started—despite the widely held belief that a clean drift is necessary. In my experience, Cowichan browns display little interest until the fly accelerates and veers from its drift. In standing waves (not whitewater) that flows over a well broken bottom, I have caught them with a fly that skittered like a water-skier.

During midsummer, when their distribution becomes somewhat unbalanced, browns are less inclined to occupy what might be considered normal trout territory. They now strongly favor big dark pools bounded by good riffles above and below. The riffles are particularly productive for large fish during the evening. The larger browns appear to have a more strongly established diurnal migration habit. It's a sort of let's-beat-it-down-to-Joe's-for-supper sort of thing.

There might be several reasons for the diurnal migration of brown trout. In addition to being sensitive to light, the brown might also be sensitive to daily temperature variations. It might be that the brown makes his evening journey in an attempt to find a more comfortable temperature. It is at least true that the shallows cool far faster than do the deep pools. It is also possible that the thermal shift triggers a movement of insects. On several occasions I have made a morning trip to the Cowichan to discover that an extensive hatch had occurred the previous night. I knew the hatch occurred at night for the simple reason that I had been on the river the previous evening, and nothing had happened up to the time I left. Light conditions might be a factor that triggers night hatches, but I think it equally likely that microshifts in water temperature also bring them on.

Today, the Cowichan has a good variety of insect hatches, although they are nothing like those reported during the 20's when the Cowichan was an unspoiled stream. The logging of the 30's did serious damage to the insects' habitat. The river became highly susceptible to floods and droughts. Records show that in one 12-month period, water flow ranged from 12,000 cubic feet per second to 12 CFS. Over the years, the Cowichan has been gradually regaining some of its insect populations. There are now good hatches of Mayflies and sedges. Stoneflies are not plentiful, but they are not plentiful on most other coastal streams of the province either. It can only be hoped that the insect situation will continue to improve.

In my view, insects are absolutely vital to the Cowichan brown trout. And I do not accept the long-standing accusations that browns are overly predacious and a threat to native species. From my observations on the Cowichan, I would argue that the brown is no more predacious than the native cutthroat. It is at least certain that the brown is primarily insectivorous.

I further believe that the brown is a quality game fish that deserves to be considered a candidate for other watersheds. There are streams, such as the Similkameen, that would probably prove to be almost as good for browns as the Cowichan. And, considering that the brown trout of the U.S. and Europe have withstood tremendous angling pressure, it might now be time to introduce them to those B.C. waters that are suited to them, and where the native trout are unable to withstand the ever-increasing take by anglers.

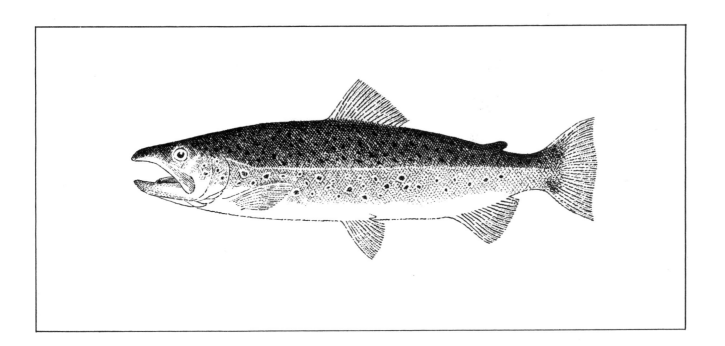

Dave Stewart

The Kokanee

I COULD ONLY stare at what appeared to be an old hook-jawed sockeye male, straight out of a Fraser River gillnet. Five pounds if an ounce. So the tales I had been hearing of big Kootenay kokanee were true.

"We've got half a dozen more, a bit smaller, down at the boat." Ian's last statement instantly brought me out of the sleeping bag, my headache and sniffles forgotten.

Photographer Tom Hall, my son Ian, and I were camping on the West Arm of Kootenay Lake, 10 miles east of Nelson. Tom and I had been poking around Duncan Dam, then under construction, to gather pictures and facts for a series I was writing about the dams. During two days of crawling about in the damp, cold diversion tunnels, I'd developed a nasty head cold.

We'd arrived at our camp late the previous night, with me sniffing and snorting like a bear on a garbage dump. Ian, who had been looking forward to the fishing part of the trip, had unsuccessfully tried to get me up at daylight. He had better results with Tom.

After seeing the fish they had caught in an hour, I suddenly became impatient. Kokanee I've seen—from many lakes across this huge old province of ours—but never had I seen such a kokanee as Ian displayed.

After downing a hasty breakfast, we set out in Tom's little alumnium cartop. Tom and Ian claimed that the action had died down, but I had never experienced anything to compare with what followed. Kokanee rose all around our anchored boat. And they were big, fat kokanee, some as large or larger than Ian's trophy.

Within two hours, casting from the cramped quarters of the anchored boat, we boated a dozen big kokanee. We used silver-red Deadly Dick wobblers, and the action came in flurries. We soon found that a cast in front of a school almost always worked, whereas a wobbler dropped directly on the school simply spooked the fish.

At first, they were near the surface. (Ian and Tom had hit their fish right on the surface, at daylight.) As the morning progressed, we had to let our lures sink deeper and deeper. By 10:30, when we quit, the fish were only occasionally taking, and were almost impossible to hook solidly.

This pattern is common enough. Kokanee are plankton-feeders. As the sun rises, especially during hot weather, plankton settles deeper in the lake. The kokanee follow it down. Lures must be fished accordingly. Investigations carried out on Lake Pend Oreille in Idaho show that, during warm weather, Kokanee usually feed at depths of 18 to 50 feet.

When we stopped, we weighed our fish. Nearly all were over four pounds; several topped five. But Ian's first big male was the largest: an even six pounds, on the resort's tested scales. Since that August day in 1966, Ian and I have made several trips to the West Arm of Kootenay Lake. Never have we been disappointed. And we have always found the Kootenay kokanee as tasty as sockeye salmon taken fresh from the saltchuck, and almost as big.

Just how the Kootenay fish managed to regain the health and vitality of their anadromous forebearers is a

61

mystery. Certainly the introduction of a fresh-water shrimp, *mysis relicta* , was one factor, but I believe there must be other reasons.

Other B.C. kokanee have exceeded the normal length of 10 to 12 inches. At one time, many Kokanee of Wood Lake (on the highway between Vernon and Kelowna) topped five pounds. Today they seldom top two pounds.

The kokanee of Canim Lake, in the central Cariboo, have exceeded three pounds. They were introduced during the 1950's to provide forage for rainbow trout and char. Conditions were so favourable to the landlocked salmon that they flourished and became important game fish in their own right.

Over the past two decades, the kokanee of Okanagan and Skaha lakes have shown a significant increase in size. The increase has roughly paralleled the increase in pollution. Phosphates have fertilized the lakes. The results can be seen in algae bloom, which turns the water varying shades of brownish-green, and turns tourist-promoters pale.

Kokanee occur naturally in all B.C. waters where sockeye salmon spawn, or did spawn in the past. And both kokanee and sockeye generally spawn in streams that feed into lakes. The lakes are the nurseries for their fry. The Babine and Shuswap systems presently support large sockeye runs. Kootenay Lake had large salmon runs prior to dam construction. Okanagan Lake had salmon runs 200 to 300 years ago, but not since the white man arrived. The Kokanee populations in lakes such as Kootenay and Okanagan are said to be landlocked. In lakes where sockeye salmon occur, there are two types of kokanee: landlocked, and residual.

Residual kokanee are offspring of anadromous sockeye salmon. After spending their first year in the lake, sockeye fry commence circling the shoreline. When they wander across the outlet of the lake, they are drawn into the current, and thus begin their oceanward journey. But not all the tiny fish make the trip. If a heavy wind happens to be blowing inland when the surface-circling fry approach the outlet, many of the fry are blown back into the lake. The fry continue circling until they again pass the outlet. If they encounter adverse winds again, they may take up residence in the lake. These residuals may be distinguished from landlocked kokanee by their dull olive grey spawning coloration. The spawning colours of the land-locked kokanee are the same as those displayed by anadromous sockeye: the body is bright red, and the heads (particularly on males) are bottle green.

Not many years back, kokanee were not rated as sport fish. The few kokanee taken were incidental to the trout or char catch, and very few anglers realized that the *little silver trout* were actually landlocked sockeye salmon. With the boom in sport fishing after the Second World War, and the concurrent upswing in the use of spinning tackle, greater numbers of kokanee were taken. But, although they now constitute a large percentage of the total catch from any lake in which they occur, kokanee still haven't received the consideration due them.

It is understandable why the kokanee gets second billing on some B.C. lakes. In Kootenay Lake, for example, the giant rainbow trout and Dolly Varden would naturally be more highly prized. But the greatest part of the Kootenay Lake catch is Kokanee. Similarly, Shuswap Lake is noted for its big Kamloops, Dolly Varden and lake trout; but it is certain that kokanee can be taken almost summer-long anywhere in the lake, and must form a significant part of the overall catch.

The kokanee of Nicola Lake, on the other hand, have already earned independent recognition. Nicola Lake resorts have long lists of anglers who make yearly kokanee-fishing trips. May and June are the busiest months. Insofar as anglers are concerned, the Nicola kokanee are probably the most obliging in the province. I have found that once I located a school I could easily catch them. Kokanee Beach, about one-third of the way down the long, narrow lake is one of the better spots.

There are literally hundreds of small lakes throughout the province where kokanee occur, either naturally or by stocking. Stocked lakes often produce astonishing catches, especially within the first decade of their planting. Ironically, in many lakes where the little redfish were introduced to provide forage for trout, they have become the dominant species.

In some lakes, the kokanee's size and habits may have made him less of a forage fish than it was initially hoped. Kootenay Lake is a prime example. Kootenay kokanee are reaching a size well beyond the normal 10 to 12 inches. Accordingly, the large rainbows and Dollies are less able to forage on them after the intended bait fish reach age two. One might ask "So what? Can't they eat the two-year olds?" Well, they do, of course, but only to a limited extent. Further, it appears that kokanee prefer the deep waters of the main lake. Young kokanee fresh from their home stream are heavily preyed upon. But once they get out of the shallows and into deeper water, they are relatively safe from both Dollies and trout—which tend to forage in the bays, inlets and other shallower water. I would hazard a guess, however, that since Kootenay trout and Dollies have increased in both size and numbers during the past decade, the Kootenay Lake kokanee is still a significant forage fish.

Of more immediate concern, is the sharp reduction in spawning grounds caused by the construction of Duncan Dam. Extensive spawning channels have been built along Meadow Creek, adjacent to the dam. So far, the channels seem to be effective. However, only time will tell whether the Meadow Creek spawning beds can hold the population at its present level.

For decades Meadow Creek has produced most of the spawn used in stocking B.C. lakes with kokanee. This brings to mind a fascinating incident. From 1949 through 1951, there was a high degree of albinism among the Meadow Creek kokanee propagated at the Summerland hatchery. Specimens were preserved and sent to the University of B.C.

Regional biologist Dave Hurn described the kokanee as being "simply beautiful. Their bellies were pure pearl-white; their sides and backs were golden. The operculum (gill covers) were especially bright, and their eyes were red, as with most albinos . . . ."

A golden salmon. What a fish that would be. And, since albinos reproduce albinos, a few years of fish culture could have developed a beautiful new strain of koka-nee that would have made B.C. famous the world over. But so much for dreams. Officially, kokanee are merely a valuable kind of feed for trout. And so long as that sort of archaic thinking persists, there is little chance that an albino strain will be developed. Of course, archaic thinking is not undemocratic. The official attitude might be summed up this way:

"We are responsible for creating the sort of fishing that today's fisherman wants; it is not our prerogative to change his wants or to create new ones."

I feel that this province's kokanee fishery is being wrongfully neglected. And I do not mean simply in terms of glamour fish as mentioned above. It is worth remembering that the kokanee provides a great deal of sport for the average angler. In many of the B.C. lakes where kokanee are indigenous, a fisherman can be reasonably certain that with a little gang-troll he can catch several lovely little fish.

This is not to say that spin-fishermen cannot take good catches. In Kootenay Lake, particularly on the West Arm, most of the catch falls to spin-fishermen. It is during the summer months—when the landlocked salmon gather prior to making their spawning runs—that cast wobblers are at their best. The wobbler should be fairly small and heavy. Preferred colours are flame-orange and silver. Brass is occasionally used. Wobblers of the Deadly Dick type are most common; the Len Thompson No. 7 and No. 00 also work well. Although I have yet to discover a fly which will take the West Arm kokanee, I still hope to.

In lakes of the Okanagan system (Wood, Okanagan, Skaha, Vaseaux and Osoyoos) trolling is by far the most productive technique. The most popular gear is a small or medium gang-troll, with a 14-inch leader and hook baited with either worms or one of the previously-mentioned kokanee lures. Sometimes lures such as Dick Nite or Kokanee-killer are effective when trolled without help from a gang-troll. The unencumbered troll also gives the comparatively small fish a better chance to display his fighting ability.

When using a gang-troll for kokanee, a rubber bumper should be placed between the troll and the leader. For years, ordinary rubber bands were used. Today's manu-factured bumpers are much handier. The rubber bumper cushions the pull between hook and gang troll. Because a kokanee has a soft mouth, he is apt to tear free when he fights hard against a near-rigid troll.

During the winter months, still-fishing is particularly worthwhile. In the West Arm of Kootenay Lake, big catches are taken during December and January. Hell-gramites or stone-fly nymphs are excellent bait, as are meal-worms or wood grubs. Small baithooks are required and the line should be weighted as lightly as practicable, as these winter feeders often take the bait very lightly. The West Arm bait fishing is done both from drifted or anchored boats and from shore. On other lakes, notably Lac La Hache, good catches are taken through the ice.

In the past, spawning kokanee were often indiscriminately slaughtered by poachers using everything from gaff-hooks and snares to dynamite. Fisheries men were kept busy trying to prevent people from literally wiping out whole runs. Happily, people are now showing more restraint. The kokanee's sport value is beginning to be appreciated.

Kokanee are easily distinguished from trout by their silvery sides (they are often called *silvers*) sharp nose, and forked tail with sharp tips. Positive identification may be made by counting the rays of the anal fin. Kokanee have 13 or more rays in this fin; trout have 12 or fewer.

In addition to being labelled silvers, kokanee are often called redfish, or little redfish. Their name has been corrupted in some localities to "kickininee." The title "redfish" stems from their coloration at spawning. Males quickly develop long hooked noses; their silver sides turn scarlet, and their heads turn bottle green. Spawning females turn a duller red shade, and they do not develop the hooked nose and humped back of the male. The spent fish drop back into deep holes where they soon die.

In most streams, spawning occurs in August. The Eagle River, west of Revelstoke, has a good run during late August and early September. So do the streams of the West Arm of Kootenay Lake. In streams near the north end of Kootenay Lake, there are two distinct and later-running races. Kokanee which spawn in the streams entering the Columbia near Revelstoke do so in September, nearly a month later than those in the headwaters of the Shuswap system just a few miles to the west.

The kokanee's life-pattern closely parallels that of the sockeye salmon. Mature fish are usually four-year-olds. Eggs deposited in the redds during September emerge as alevin during February. Alevins move downstream until they reach backwaters or sloughs, where they spend their first year. Freshets of the following spring urge them downstream to the lake where they feed and grow.

During their two years in the lake, kokanee stay offshore (in the deepest water), feeding entirely upon plankton and the small organisms called zooplankton. As they approach maturity, they move closer to the surface. During late summer, they can often be seen in large schools. Maturing kokanee quite frequently break the surface in skipping jumps—as do sockeye salmon. There seems to be no good reason for the jumping; they certainly aren't taking food when they make those long, sideways skips. It might be that they are reacting to imminent and violent metabollic changes. Perhaps it's their way of preparing themselves for the long, final trek to the spawning grounds where they die in the very process of giving life.

Jim Kilburn

The Rainbow Trout

THE SMALL TRUCK crawled up the hill. At the top, the driver climbed out to stretch his legs. He had been on that narrow, twisting, deep-rutted road since midnight. He needed a pause.

In the early light, he could distinguish little on the hills that rolled one upon the other out of sight. But he knew he must be close to the lake he sought. He knew from the miles he had driven.

It wasn't until he turned to get back into the truck that he looked behind—and down. There, nestled in a meadow, was a small lake, calm and grey. Could this be Reed Lake? He looked for the identifying features. Dawn was rapidly approaching.

First he spotted a small dam. Then he looked west of the dam for the greenery of mixed alder and birch. He had been told that it was the only stand of trees in the graze-land valley. But he saw little greenery, only a copse of long-dead trees. Could these be the skeletons of alders and birches? In the gathering light, he spotted a scar-like ribbon linking the dam and the now-dead trees. This could only be a creek bed. Now he was certain.

He had heard Reed Lake described a dozen times, by a dozen anglers. And each time he had heard talk of the lake's giant rainbow trout. But all that was long past. It was part of his youth. Now he was a seasoned angler. Yet, despite the fact that he hadn't heard of trout taken there for more than half a generation, he had good reason to search for Reed Lake.

The innocent-looking dam had been the cause of the lake's sudden decline. Built to raise the lake level so that range cattle could water from firm ground, it also barred the mature rainbows from the outlet stream. In a few short years, the last of the lake's mature, red-flanked trout had died—unspawned in the shallows.

As he climbed back into the truck, he was suddenly conscious of how soon he might discover whether or not his hunch was right. He'd heard that lakes in the area had been stocked by aircraft two years earlier. If the rumor were true, and if Reed Lake had received a planting, he might be mere minutes away from great fishing.

He hadn't much time to think before he reached the end of the road. But even before gathering his tackle and launching his small boat, he had considered several questions. What if the lake were no longer rich in trout feed? What if too many or too few trout had been stocked? What age and size were the planted fish? How much could they be expected to grow in two years?

After loading his tackle, he lighted a cigarette. He carefully eased out from shore, as if reluctant to disturb the prevading calm. His oars dipped, then lifted, stirring the shoreline weed. In so doing, one of his questions was answered. For there, quietly churning in the wake of the oar blade, were several dozen, greenish, inch-long shrimp.

Newly hopeful, he decided to row to the outlet end of the lake. During Reed Lake's heyday, the shoals there had been particularly productive. He knew the lake was now changed, but he would watch for signs as he rowed. He fully expected to see evidence of feeding trout. After all, the oldtimers had spoken of Reed Lake trout feeding at three distinct periods during the day—morning, noon, and evening. He was on hand for their breakfast hour.

From the oldtimers' yarns, he knew that Reed Lake trout moved shoalward when they fed, and that when they fed, they nearly always showed. Sometimes—as they searched for snails in a few inches of water—their broad, spotted tails would break the surface. Sometimes—as they rose to surface insects—they would swirl or porpoise. Sometimes—as they fed just under the surface—they would create the smallest of tell-tale bulges or whirlpools.

By the time he reached the outlet end of the lake, the sun was on the water. But he had seen no sign. Undaunted, he anchored along an abrupt drop-off near the dam.

Like so many others who flyfish for lake rainbows, he carried three rods. One was rigged with a high-density line for deep fishing; one a sink-tip line for midwater fishing, and the third a floating line for surface and near-surface fishing. He began with the high-density line and a number 10 Green Shrimp.

The sun was past its zenith when he lifted anchor to row ashore. He'd had no strikes. He hadn't even seen a sign of fish. For the first time, he seriously began to doubt.

He pulled his small boat onto the grassy shore, paused a few moments, then manoeuvred his way through the sun-baked cakes of cow-dung. As he approached the outlet stream, he began wondering—as he so often had—why

Reed Lake's trout had been so big.

An hour later, he was once again rowing. This time he went directly to the middle of the lake where he periodically lowered his anchor to take soundings. At the shoal near his chosen campsite, he again stirred the weed with his oar. For a long while he silently studied the shallows.

He was deep in thought as he went ashore. Almost mechanically, he pitched his tent and cooked a meal. He decided that, barring an unforseen happenstance, he would not fish again until dusk. He didn't expect the trout—if there were any in Reed Lake—to feed till then. However, he did spend the remaining afternoon hours on the lake. He explored, sounded, watched. By the time he returned to camp for his evening meal, he had collected his thoughts. He was reasonably certain why Reed Lake had once grown giant trout.

He was convinced that Reed Lake trout had resulted from a series of ecological accidents. The lake was small —less than half a square mile. From his soundings, he estimated the lake to be no deeper than 40 feet. It was well sheltered from wind, and had no inlet stream. In all likelihood, it was fed only by seepage and groundwater. Though now only a trickle, he was certain that the outlet stream was once of a fair size.

Below the dam, the stream had dropped abruptly—for a short distance. In so doing, it had cut a straight, deep swath through the grazeland. The tumbling stream had scattered coarse gravel downstream of the lake outlet for

several hundred yards. From that point, the land sloped more gradually, and the streambed assumed a wandering course through a meadow to the now-familiar stand of alder and birch.

From a distance, it looked as if all the trees were dead. Closer inspection showed that the alder and birch adjoining the now-shrivelled stream were still alive. And, in some places, quiet pools hinted at the one-time nature of the stream. The gravel suggested good spawning conditions. Doubtless, the pools of the alder thicket once had been bigger. But even in the past they must have been shaded and relatively gently-flowing—ideal nursery grounds for young rainbows.

Although he felt positive that the stream had once been a busy rearing area for rainbows, he felt equally certain that Reed Lake was simply too small, too shallow, and too sheltered to permit a large survival of trout. It was of a size and depth that encouraged both heavy, prolonged ice-cover in winter, and dense, choking algae-bloom in summer. Without sufficient wind to charge the lake with oxygen, it was unlikely that many trout had survived either critical period. Doubtless the trout that did survive had fed well, and grown quickly—if the super-concentration of shoal feed was any indication.

Thinking back, he realized that the oldtimers had never mentioned abundances of big trout. He had merely assumed that. The oldtimers had always emphasized the quality, not the quantity of Reed Lake rainbows. Perhaps the outlet stream had been able to produce the surpluses necessary to compensate for the harsh lake conditions. Perhaps the draw-off of the outlet stream had created a mild current that caused oxygen to concentrate in the shallows at the outlet end of the lake. Perhaps the thrice-daily visit of the big rainbows to that particular area was prompted as much by a search for oxygen as it was by a search for food.

To carry the speculation one step further, it might have been that the critical conditions of the lake drove many trout into the more oxygenated riffles of the creek itself. If this were even remotely true, and if Reed had been recently stocked, trout in the present dammed-up lake were in even greater peril. In realizing that planted trout had little chance for survival in Reed Lake, he suddenly felt saddened.

Standing quietly and sadly at the shore, he gazed lazily at the unruffled and now-unpromising surface. His bright hopes dimmed with the setting sun. He reached into the boat, picked up one of his rods, and began to dismantle it. Then, as if ashamed at surrendering so easily, he reseated the ferrule.

No sooner had he done so when a trout swirled at the edge of the dropoff—almost within casting distance. The swirl left a huge inky depression in the quiet surface. Slowly the depression filled till only a concentric circle of small waves remained. Somehow he couldn't move. Then another fish swirled. This one was farther along the dropoff, and it broke the spell. He quickly got into the small boat, still not quite able to believe it all.

A third trout swirled—or was there only one trout? Each had risen in an identical manner. He selected the rod that was rigged with the weight-forward, sink-tip line. He false cast the heavy portion of the line past the rod tip, coiled a long length of shooting line on the boat's floor boards, and waited.

Again a swirl. About 30 feet from the boat. He false cast twice, to get the line airborne, then sent the shooting line rapping through the guides. No sooner had the small shrimp pattern alighted at the edge of the swirl than a fish showed twenty feet beyond. This time he was certain; it was the same fish, and it was moving rapidly. He cast about thirty feet ahead of the last rise, hoping to put the fly in the trout's pathway.

He allowed the fly to settle for several seconds before he began to recover line in slow, arm-length strips. The fish took going away. The rod tip bounced onto the water. The reel screamed. There was a slight pause when the reel stopped. Then the trout broke the surface. Neither the distance nor the gathering dark could hide the fact that it was a big fish. Again and again the fish leaped. The sounds of his jumps echoed across the nighttime stillness.

By the time the fish faltered, the moon had already made considerable progress in its slow rise across the dark sky. As if in sympathy with the moon, the rainbow gleamed its own silver from the boatside depths. The fish was obviously tired; it was rolling on its side more and more frequently. At long last it was beside the boat, on its side, big and bright. And clearly too large for the net.

The angler carefully held the leader in his left hand. He then placed the reel on the centre seat and the rod point over the side of the boat. Equally carefully, he reached for the trout in an attempt to lift it into the boat. At his finger's touch, the trout made a final bid for freedom. The angler made a desperate attempt for his rod, but was too late.

He stayed at Reed Lake three more days, fishing hard and long. Somehow, he wasn't disappointed that he'd hooked but one fish, and that he'd lost that fish. He wasn't even disappointed that he had seen no other fish move. He simply wasn't expecting anything more.

At the crest of the hill where he had stopped four days

earlier, he once again got out of his truck. It was a final look. The water was still unruffled. He climbed into the truck thinking of those who had fished there in the past. And he felt akin to them, for in one moonlit hour, he had shared both their triumphs and their disappointments. What more could he ask?

THE RAINBOW TROUT, once exclusively a resident of Western North America, now thrives in waters the world over. But despite the fact that the rainbow is known and respected globally, there is still no better place to fish for him than in the province of British Columbia. And the rainbow is clearly the most sought-after sportfish in this province.

Although some academics would argue that rainbow and steelhead trout (both labelled *Salma gairdneri* by scientific folk) and the Atlantic salmon (*Salmo salar*) are related, anglers generally regard the rainbow as the largest true trout. And, although *Field and Stream Magazine*, the self-appointed judge of world-record sportfish, lists a 37-pounder from Pend Oreille (Idaho) as the largest ever, B.C.'s small Jewel Lake (in the Grand Forks-Greenwood district) once produced far heftier rainbows. The largest Jewel Lake rainbow measured 36 inches and weighed 52½ pounds.

Rainbows that migrate to the sea lose their rainbow status; they are called steelhead, and steelhead will not be considered here. It's enough to consider rainbows that remain true to fresh water.

Providing they don't taste the sea, coastal rainbows are inevitably referred to as rainbows. Which is right and proper. But, in the interior of the province, particularly in the Kamloops region, rainbows are often called Kamloops trout—which may or may not be a clever ploy of the Kamloops tourist lobby.

Those anglers who claim there is a distinction say that the Kamloops is more silvery than the rainbow. But colouration is an unreliable indication; like other differences, colour is often merely a result of environment or condition. Rainbows in shallow, dark, or acidic lakes are more inclined to be dark. Mature rainbows (four or five years of age) likewise tend to be highly coloured. Immature, or *maiden* rainbows, particularly those in deep, clear, or alkaline lakes, are often as silvery as fresh-run salmon or steelhead. Such rainbows are firm of flesh, stubby in shape, bluish above the lateral line, silvery on the sides, and white on the belly. The belly fins are often a cloudy white. The spotting is moderate, X-shaped, and mostly above the lateral line. Both the tail and dorsal fins are heavily spotted, and a few round spots occur on top

of the head and behind the eye. The faintly iridescent pink stripe that follows the lateral line from gill plate to tail is also a decidedly attractive feature. Such rainbows are indeed quality fish.

As the spawning season approaches, the rainbow's pink stripe darkens to red, and his silvery sides turn greyish. He also becomes more heavily spotted. A spawning male may be extremely dark along his entire belly—from jaw to tail. His gill plates may be bright red, and his jaws considerably lengthened and hooked. In this condition, he is of little interest to discriminating anglers. Naturally, every angler has his preference. The discriminating angler looks for the prime-conditioned fish that look well, taste well, and fight well.

Pound for pound few sportfish fight as well as the interior rainbow. And, because he fights, runs and leaps so well, a rainbow is quickly exhausted. Even so, a 10-minute battle is enough to leave an angler shaken. The rainbow is seldom a quitter. Even when exhausted and apparently ready for the net, he will often rally.

The rainbow is native to most B.C. watersheds—from Stuart Lake in the north to Kootenay Lake in the south, and from the west coast to the Rocky Mountains. And in many watersheds where he did not naturally occur, he has been stocked. Planted rainbows are frequently trucked or airlifted to their destinations. Many stocked lakes that have no spawning facilities, teem with aquatic feed. In such food-rich environments, the planted trout may grow quickly. To do so, plantings must be carefully controlled so that the introduced trout do not over-balance the food chain. In several lakes, fish biologists have been able to control the average trout size. It is possible for highly-productive lakes to perpetually support a high percentage of large, well-conditioned rainbows.

There are few lakes of such quality in B.C. However, there are numerous lakes that provide sporadic but high-quality fishing. Such fishing usually results from experimental or indiscriminate plantings. In some cases, initial plantings overbalanced the lake's food chain. The planted trout thrived on the super-abundant larder—but only for a brief period. All too quickly the trout depleted the larder. Trout of following plantings could only be smaller. In other cases, plantings initially balanced the food supply. This resulted in a more durable quality fishery. When such a lake is either overstocked or overlooked, however, a sharp degeneration in both size and condition of trout results. Because of these and other imponderables, the discriminating angler must know his fishing area well. Otherwise he'll have difficulty finding the big rainbow that are so casually mentioned in tourist brochures.

70

To date, quality fishing has been of little concern to the Provincial government. Officials of the Province's Fish Branch cry that they have neither funds nor personnel to establish such a specialized fishery. Dedicated anglers reply that the Branch simply hasn't the desire to do so. Many coastal fishermen charge the Branch with focussing on interior rainbows because the Branch either lacks the know-how or the political strength to do anything for coastal steelhead. Whatever the cause, it is a certainty that B.C. anglers are becoming increasingly aware of the need for quality fishing. Perhaps only a quality Fish Branch could recognize that need.

The present branch recently made a timid gesture by designating that on three Merritt area lakes—Peterhope, Salmon, and Pennask—only flyfishing will be permitted. Although this is a step forward, it is still woefully inadequate. This province is long overdue for both quality thinking and quality fishing regulations. It is doubtful that there can ever be quality fishing on small-acreage lakes until organic baits, outboard motors (other than electric) and ice-fishing are outlawed. Such regulations would largely eliminate the need for legislation such as fly-only water.

Meanwhile, there is little to protect quality lakes. Highly-productive lakes are currently being overplanted —to provide large numbers of small trout for tourists. Ice-fishing is almost encouraged—even on lakes where the evidence suggests it should be banned. And ice-fishing goes unchecked—legal limits are seldom observed, or enforced. Many experienced trout fishermen say that, in certain areas, big rainbows are now harder than ever to find after each ice-out. Even worse, ice fishermen who use live bait have all too frequently introduced undesirable species of coarse fish into lakes. The coarse fish compete with trout for the food supply. Many lakes having coarse fish have already been poisoned. This, the first step in rehabilitating a lake, causes the lake to be lost to anglers for several years.

It is both costly and stupid that such a trouble-making style of fishing is permitted on small lakes. Consider, too, the damage done by motor boats on small lakes. Large motor boats, such as the types used in water-skiing, are particularly odious. They disturb both fisherman and fish. They pollute the surface with oil and gasoline, which may create far greater havoc among aquatic insects than we can now understand.

It's been pointed out that oil desposits are already inhibiting insect emergences, particularly on small lakes. Outboarders have bleated that because interior rainbows largely feed on bottom organisms (or small landlocked Kokanee, where available), that the loss of a few aquatic insects would be of little account. Perhaps. But it is a certainty that emerging insects are important to the angler. They are directly responsible for some of the Interior's most spectacular fishing. Without them, where would fly-fishing be? Any decline in aquatic insects must therefore affect the quality of interior trouting.

Until quality fishing is a fact, anglers can only search and hope. Perhaps they will be lucky enough, as I was last year, to find a small lake that had been forgotten by both ice-fishers and fishery-biologists. Perhaps then, as I did last year, they will enjoy a few quiet days of fishing, with nothing to disturb the stillness but the sigh of the reeds, the swish of the line, and the rise of big interior rainbows.

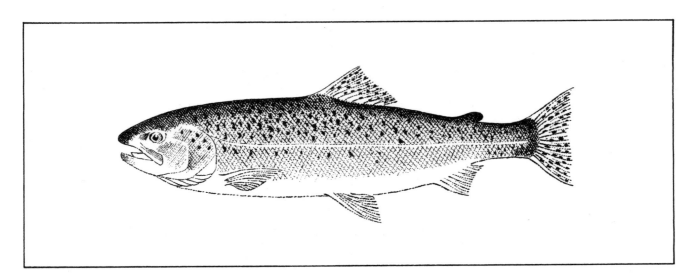

Pete Broomhall

The Coho Salmon

Like the other Pacific salmon, cohoes begin and end their lives in freshwater, have a range that extends from California to Alaska, and are both big enough and fast enough to rank highly on the scale of desirable sport fish. But the coho deserves particular respect. Not only do sportfishermen catch more cohoes than any other species, but they catch them by a greater variety of fishing methods. Furthermore, on a pound-for-pound basis, the coho is the scrappiest, jumpiest salmon of them all.

The coho begins his life inauspiciously enough as an egg in the gravel of a stream or river. As he begins to assume fish form, he also begins to stir in his gravel womb. Soon he fights his way upward through the gravel to face the dangers of stream life. The young coho usually leaves freshwater in the spring of his second year. As a sea-going migrant, he is usually less than four inches in length.

In the sea, the coho finds the abundance that quickly transforms him into sportfish stature. By late spring of his second year, he weighs two to four pounds. He is then called a blueback. And, even as a blueback, he is a worthy sport fish—provided he is taken on tackle that is not too heavy to drown his fighting ability. During the blueback stage—May is a reasonable guess—the coho switches from a diet of shrimp and such-like to needlefish and herring. By mid-summer, he generally tops five pounds—the traditionally-accepted division between blueback and coho. He is then truly a suitable target for sportfishermen. From the spring, through the summer, and into autumn, he continues to feed on herring. And during that four- to five-month period he may quadruple his weight.

By late summer or early autumn, many cohoes weigh from 10 to 20 pounds. The world record, an even 31-pounder, was taken on October 11, 1947, from Cowichan Bay on Vancouver Island. It was taken by a veteran saltchucker, Mrs. Patty Hallberg. The big fish, caught during a fishing derby, was initially misidentified as a spring salmon. Later it was positively identified as a coho, the largest ever taken by either sport- or commercial-fishing methods. It was caught on the then-popular Tillicum plug, fought for 20 minutes, and topped the previous world-record by five pounds.

Cowichan Bay is no longer particularly renowned as a big-coho haunt. Today it is the Queen Charlotte Islands that grab the limelight. During recent years, a considerable number of 20-plus-pounders have been boated there. Saltchuckers have also taken many trophy-sized cohoes from the Bamfield area on Vancouver Island's west coast, and freshwater buffs have landed lunkers in the Skeena watershed. (It is widely held that the true heavyweights are four-year-old fish, one year older than is normal for cohoes.)

By October, the spawning migration is well under way. Few mature cohoes remain in the sea as late as November, and those which do have generally lost their sea-silver appeal. The hazards of the upstream migration need no chronicling here. What might be more to the point is to mention that even though cohoes do not feed while making their spawning run, they can still be taken by sportfishing techniques.

In many respects, the upstream-bound coho offers the best possible sport. He is at his maximum weight; he is somewhat harder to manage in river currents than he is in the sea; and river-fishing tackle is almost always light enough to permit him to put on a good performance. Against this is the fact that upstream cohoes soon lose their sea-silver shine; and as they darken and ripen, they lose both attractiveness and vigour.

By the time cohoes reach some rivers they are already too coloured to be of interest to sportfishermen. And, on most other rivers, the coho season is quite short. Few rivers have runs of clean coho for more than four to six weeks. And that's one of the sad things about the decline and fall of the streams on Vancouver's North Shore. Those streams were unique in having good runs of fresh, sea-bright cohoes spaced over about five months of the year. In years past, the North Shore coho season got underway in late June and continued right through October. (I have taken clean North Shore cohoes as early as May 10, and as late as December 3. Doubtless there are others who have taken them both earlier and later.)

In those happier bygone times, light-tackle float-fishing was very much in vogue. The method is as valid today as it was then, particularly in clear-flowing smallish rivers. Rods were nine to ten feet in length, and of a lighter action than the nine- and ten-foot sticks commonly used today. Even as late as the early fifties, many—if not most —of the rods were made of split cane. Single-action revolving drum reels of the Hardy Silex variety were popular, but many enthusiasts used nothing but large fly reels, the Hardy St. John being the number one choice. Lines of 12-pound test nylon monofilament, and leaders from four- to eight-pound test were about average. The lines of those halycon days were harder and less evenly drawn than are today's lines. One of those old four-pound-test leaders could often take strains in excess of six pounds. Equally often they would snap at a four-pound pull. Line ratings were simply geared to the lowest breaking strain that could be expected to occur. Understandably, the beaching of a fresh-run salmon took as much dexterity then as it does now.

By and large, terminal gear is still rigged in the same manner. The float was adjusted to keep the bait barely off the bottom. (It is noticeable that anglers who served their apprenticeship on the North Shore streams tend to use smaller floats than are commonly used.) Two, three, or four SSG split shot were spaced along a four-foot leader. The first shot was 18 to 24 inches from the hook; the remainder about six inches apart. Because both leader and rod-tip were fine, smaller hooks were used in those days. A number two was considered big, a number four or six average, and thin-wire shiner hooks not uncommon. When medium or small hooks were used, they were often tied in tandem, or in series. (Some ardents tied as many as five shiner hooks over a four-inch space.) Invariably, dew worms were used as bait.

One of the Capilano River's most picturesque summertime coho pools was just above tidewater. It was called the Stump Hole in recognition of one huge stump at the head of the pool, and a large, uprooted, and half-buried tree that split the river at the tail end. When the incoming tide was high enough, the rapids at the pool's tail end all but disappeared. Sometimes a single roll of water separated river from sea.

High tides were particularly important when the river was low. The filling estuary encouraged the cohoes to venture upstream over an otherwise very thinly covered riverbed. The Stump Hole was at its best when a high tide came in the evening of a sunny summer day. Shadows cast by the westbank trees seemed to give the cohoes the additional assurance they needed. On such occasions it was quite commonplace to see the salmon cross the shallows separating river and sea. And, on such occasions, it was not uncommon for a half-dozen or more oldtimers to be on hand to greet the fish.

The oldtimers would space themselves along the east bank, taking turns casting. Their floats would bob downstream in a single-file line—just to one side of the main current. Because it was a fairly long drift, there was time enough to sneak glances at the other fellow's floats—just to see if anyone was getting an offer—or to peer into the gin-clear depths in an attempt to spot the cohoes. Now and then a coho would flash as it turned on its side. Sometimes the fish did that when grazed by a leader. At other times they seemed merely to be responding to some unfathomable ministrations of the river.

Occasionally, a downriver glance would catch a glimpse of a seal, for in those days there were salmon enough to attract the seals well into the estuary. Or, as I once saw, a coho struggling upstream despite missing a fist-sized chunk of silver underbelly. He didn't quite have the strength to make it into the Stump Hole before he died. The freshness of the wound was evidence that his fatal encounter with one of the estuary seals had occurred only moments before.

I have memories aplenty of the Stump Hole, and of float fishing for coho salmon. Of silver-bright, fresh-from-

the-ocean cohoes racing and jumping at the end of my line, or at the end of lines cast by others. But of all I remember, nothing remains clearer than the first salmon I ever saw taken. It was a five-pounder, and it came from the Stump Hole in September. I was twelve, and until that moment I thought that fishing was a rather useless pastime. An older brother who already liked fishing had talked me into accompanying him on a bicycle ride to the Capilano River. We left our bicycles in the bush by Marine Drive Bridge. There was only a single span crossing the river in those days, and the river had not yet been bulldozed in the name of flood control. My brother wanted to look into the deep pool directly beneath the bridge, but I was impatient with that sort of dalliance. So, sandwich lunches in hand, we hiked downstream.

Just above the Stump Hole the river split. I wasn't even much interested in wading the cold channel, but my brother said there was a good lunch-eating spot just on the other side. Because I judged eating to be a good pastime, I soon had my shoes and socks off, and my pants rolled up. We waded the channel, put our shoes back on, walked a few yards through a stand of small riverbank trees, and arrived at the Stump Hole.

As if timed for our arrival, the five-pounder chose that moment to take a float-fished dew worm belonging to one of the two fishermen on hand. It just so happened that it was a father-son team, and that it was the boy who hooked the salmon. I immediately determined in favour of fishing. "If that kid can catch a fish like that," my reasoning went, "then so can I."

For several years thereafter, my brother and I roamed

at will in a richly rewarding fishing ground. We primarily float-fished, and to satisfy our curiosity, we explored the Capilano, Lynn, and Seymour rivers from top to bottom. We found even better coho-fishing pools than the Stump Hole, and we were lucky enough to have made our discoveries during a happy period in the history of North Shore sport fishing. The coho runs are now much smaller, and most of the good pools have long since been destroyed. For these reasons, when I am serious about coho fishing, I now go elsewhere.

In my wanderings I sometimes stumble onto some fair river fishing for cohoes, but few rivers could ever compare with the Capilano of the past. And for this reason, I now do most of my coho fishing in the sea. I have trolled, mooched, stripcast, bucktailed, and spun for cohoes. I have used herring, needlefish, plugs, spoons, bucktail streamers, spinning lures, and Buzzbombs. I have fished with light tackle, and with dodger and 10-ounce sinkers. But, when I have my choice, I spin, bucktail, or Buzzbomb.

And, like many other Vancouverites, I often fish the waters off Vancouver Island's east coast. My most memorable bucktailing experiences have occurred right at Qualicum Beach. I have particularly fond memories of a morning's fishing in late September. It was overcast. The sea was flat and grey. But the cohoes did their best to brighten things. And they did it best in the bay at the mouth of Little Qualicum River. Doubtless they were there in preparation for their upstream migration. But, because there had been no rain for a couple of weeks, the river was too low to entice them upstream. Here and there a coho swirled at the surface. And here and there, saltchucker and salmon traded line. And best of all, it was a day for the surface-trolled streamer.

For me, it had to be a quick search. I was due back in Vancouver that afternoon. Consequently, when a boat rental operator said fishing seemed fair, I didn't even bother to change into fishing clothes. I simply donned a fishing jacket over shirt and tie, and jumped aboard. Several cohoes had been taken by the time I reached the bay. Almost immediately, a six-pounder took my green-and-white bucktail. That one fish would have pleased me sufficiently, but as luck would have it, others were to follow.

The salmon were slowly cruising around the perimeter of the bay. The trick was to cross ahead of a school hoping the streamer would swing into their path. For some reason or other the cohoes seemed anxious to hug the shoreline. Normally, that would present a problem. But, trolling without sinkers permits fishing in very

75

shallow water. Sometimes I was only a stone's throw off the beach. And that's where the best fishing was. The second salmon—a 10-pound spring as it turned out—took in the shallows, raced for deeper water, and fought stubbornly there for about 15 minutes. But it was the on-shore cohoes that proved the most thrilling.

Cohoes seem particularly nervous when hooked in shallow water—which is natural enough. It is equally natural that their first rush would be in a seaward direction. And that's how the Qualicum cohoes behaved. The end of their first long run was usually punctuated by one or more clean leaps. For me, a leaping coho is always a heart-stopping thing. About half the fish I tangled with that day came unstuck during a leap, and this was despite the fact that they struck hard, going away. There was no mistaking the take; the reel simply started to scream as the fish raced for deeper water.

Qualicum is not particularly noted for big cohoes, but I did manage one of 13 pounds and lost another that certainly would have bettered that mark. The big coho had caused several anxious moments, but in due course was at boatside. Everything seemed under control until I stepped forward to pass the rod tip around the bow of the small rental boat. Somehow, the laces of my street shoes managed to get tangled in the net. I tried vainly to shake the net free. Doubtless I looked like the village idiot, standing there on one foot shaking what appeared to be a snowshoe on the other. The coho chose that moment to make a leap. It was clearly a male fish, complete with hooked nose. And he was as full bodied and silver as could be wished. He was hard against the bow when he jumped. I don't know if he came unpinned on the way up or on the way down, but the suddenly slack line told me we were no longer communicating.

When fishing is good, lost fish soon are forgotten. The next coho took scant minutes after I had christened a new streamer. This fish, like the 13-pounder, was a female. I was back at the boat rental within three hours of starting out, and I had been lucky enough to boat a full limit: three cohoes—six, 12, and 13 pounds—and one 10-pound spring. The boat rental attendant discovered the bucktail streamer that I had "lost" to the bow-jumper. It was hanging from the boat's bow ring. Evidently the big coho had managed to thread the trailer hook through the ring—either on his way up or on his way down. That was all he needed to pull free from the main hook. Even apart from my foot-fault, I somehow think he deserved his freedom.

My most memorable spin-casting experiences have also occurred on the east coast of Vancouver Island. And,

again, they have taken place late in the season, when the cohoes have gathered preparatory to making their upstream run. Predictably, I have had the best results at river mouths—notably at the mouth of Salmon River at Kelsey Bay.

I've used a variety of lures, from the old Devon Minnows and tee spinners to the Buzzbomb. Today I seldom use anything but the Crocodile, Deadly Dick and Buzzbomb. Each comes in a variety of finishes; I lean toward the nickle for the Crocodile and Deadly Dick, and the natural lead-coloured finish for the Buzzbomb. There's nothing particularly tricky about fishing either the Crocodile or the Deadly Dick, but the Buzzbomb deserves a few words of explanation. It looks like a lead sinker, and it's heavy enough to cast to those cohoes that would otherwise be just out of casting range—a remarkably helpful feature. And, although it is usually fished in a lift-and-flutter manner in deepish water, it can also be very effective when fished more conventionally. I have found it particularly useful when fishing for skittish cohoes, even in shallow water.

Because I use a light seven-foot fibreglass spinning rod and eight-pound-test line when spinning for cohoes, I have found it wise to avoid making jerky casts, especially when using the heavy Buzzbomb. (Incidentally, for best casting results, the line on a spinning reel should be loaded to about one-sixteenth inch from the spool lip.) I have also found it wise to use both durable reels—a Quick Finessa is outstanding—and very sharp treble hooks.

Doubtless there are other attractive places, but for me the mouth of Salmon River is unbeatable. For one thing, the cohoes there tend to be somewhat larger than their southern cousins. The only 16-pound-plus coho salmon I have even boated came from Kelsey Bay. I've fished there a number of times now, and to my mind the best period is late September through early October. Of course, much depends both on the height of the river and the nature of the coho run.

When the tide is slack on a calm day, one can merely drift lazily at the rivermouth, only infrequently moving to new locations. When the river, or wind, or tide act up, it is often better to anchor along the dropoff. And if the salmon are there, they usually make themselves known. And sometimes the fishing is truly phenomenal.

On most of my Kelsey Bay trips, I have been fortunate enough to share the boat with two good companions. On several occasions we have battled three fish simultaneously. And on several occasions we have shared the area with a pod of killer whales. The whales never did seem anxious to try for the cohoes; they simply passed quietly through, now and then surfacing and blowing.

Perhaps the cohoes will continue to return to the Salmon River for several more years. Perhaps I will share a boat with good companions, and share the fishing grounds with killer whales for several more years also. Perhaps there will be more happy memories of October evenings anchored at the rivermouth. Of the dark sea and sky frequently being brightened by the silver-sided flashings and jumpings of prime coho salmon. Of strong-running and frantic-leaping cohoes at the end of a line.

Of salmon crossing the bar to make their exploratory forays into the river channel—tempted, no doubt, by the river being newly sweetened by the first autumn rains. Of a fishing trip's best-ever conclusion: a bottle of cool beer and a feed of freshly-caught fish, shared with friends. Perhaps if no longer at Salmon River, all this will be available elsewhere. But, if sport fishing is to be a thing of the past, if cohoes are to join the many other creatures of nature that are no more, if man insists on wasting that which makes life worthwhile, there will still be memories. That much can never be taken away.

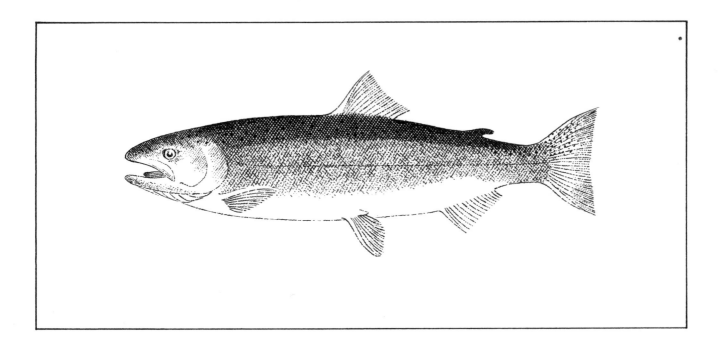

Harry Lomax

The Arctic Grayling

I WAS WARM, frustrated, and not a little embarrassed. The warmth was created by the action of wielding a fly rod for two hours under the rapidly increasing heat of a June sun. The frustration came from the fact that during the period I had yet to get even a half-hearted strike, while the embarrassment stemmed from my own admission to my companions that I was a fair fly fisherman. At that moment those two worthies occupied comfortable positions in the bottom of our 30-foot river boat, anchored at the edge of a little back eddy on the Pack River. Between disparaging remarks as to the fishing ability of newcomers to the area (me), they were rapidly consuming a half dozen iced beer and a particularly attractive lunch (both mine).

Ken Melville was the owner of Melville Lodge on Tudyah Lake, about 100 miles north of Prince George. Dick Corless, who unfortunately passed away a few years ago, at that time was freighting on the rivers making up the headwaters of the Arctic watershed. Each was an expert in his field, and like many men who spend their waking hours in the outdoors, they both possessed a great sense of humour, which at that moment I did not particularly appreciate. I was their guest, invited along on my first trip for Arctic grayling. Fortunately they took pity on the newcomer, otherwise it could well have been my last trip, and this chapter would never have been written.

With a sigh Ken heaved himself off the lifejacket that had been serving as a pillow, and picked up his flyrod.

"First thing you have to learn," he grunted between pulls at a particularly strong cigar, "is that you aren't fishing for trout." Up to that point I had serious doubts that I was fishing for anything, so I was quite prepared to listen. "Right now," my instructor continued, "grayling are getting ready to spawn, and they are not in the main stream you have been flogging, but are laying up against those flooded willows, right about there." The first cast rolled out, there was a flurry, and I got my first look at an Arctic grayling.

Almost twenty years have passed since that first memorable trip, and since that time I have developed quite an affinity for the province's least known game fish. In fact the grayling and I have been, if not good friends, at least better than nodding acquaintances.

As its name would suggest, the species is found only in cold northern streams, mainly in the Arctic watershed. In British Columbia, the Arctic watershed's southerly source is Summit Lake, 35 miles north of Prince George, largest city in the north half of the province and one of the fastest growing communities in Canada.

From Summit Lake a series of lakes and rivers flow ever northward into the Arctic Ocean; rivers like the Peace and Parsnip. These were the highways for British Columbia's early explorers. Intrepid men like Fraser and MacKenzie travelled this route in their search for the Pacific. Here was Fort MacLeod, the first post established by the Northwest Company in the province. In fact, some of the old buildings still stand. However, since that brief period of activity, the area has been pretty well taken over by men freighting on the river, and the occasional prospector and trapper. Its inhabitants also include moose, and of course, my friend the grayling. It is only comparatively recently that there has been anything like easy access to the grayling's home. Other than the native residents, very few sportsmen fished for them, and for this reason the sporting little fellow with the big fin is virtually unknown among the majority of anglers.

Although I have dwelt here in the areas where grayling can be found in British Columbia, this does not mean that the fish is limited to the province. There is excellent grayling fishing in Alaska and the Yukon. In fact, most of the streams crossing the Alaska Highway are well populated with them. Atlin Lake produces some real whoppers, and there must be literally hundreds of other lakes having grayling.

The Arctic grayling's range extends east from the Yenesei River watershed in the Soviet Union to the Churchill River on the Hudson Bay. They occur naturally in the Athabasca and Churchill drainages in Alberta, and have been introduced into the North Saskatchewan system. In B.C., graylings have been taken from the Peace-Mackenzie, Liard-Mackenzie, and Yukon systems. They have also crossed the continental divide into some Pacific drainages of the north, and have been recorded in Cold Fish Lake, parts of the Stikine and Taku river systems, and parts of the upper Alsek River system in the Yukon Territory.

If the North were ever to adopt a national fish, in the same manner as we adopt animals, birds and flowers, the natural choice would be the Arctic grayling.

There were originally three species of grayling native to North America. The Michigan grayling is now extinct, a victim of pollution and destruction of the clear cold waters that all the species demand. The Montana grayling is still found in that state and also in Wyoming. I have heard that this strain has also been introduced into the south eastern corner of B.C., but have never fished for them there. By far the most common is the Arctic grayling, and it is this particular species that is found at virtually the same latitude from close to the Pacific to Hudson's Bay.

The European species, *Thymallus Thymallus*, is very similar to the Arctic grayling, inhabits northern streams, and has long been recognized as an excellent sport fish, particularly on the fly.

Now let us take a look at the fish itself. If anyone ever starts handing out prizes for the most beautiful fresh-water fish, the grayling will certainly be among the contenders. With the possible exception of the golden trout, it is the most beautiful fish that swims. The head is a combination of blue and dark bronze. The back is blue, fading into lighter purplish blue sides, shot with silver. (Spawning males are blackish.) There are usually a few small black spots on the forepart of the body. The pectoral fins, particularly during the spawning period, are edged with orange and white. However, the most spectacular portion of the fish's anatomy is the huge dorsal fin. The upper half of this appendage has a greenish cast and it is dotted with brilliant red or purple spots. In the water, as the fish swirls, it looks more like some underwater butterfly than a member of the aquatic family. Unfortunately the colors fade once the fish leaves the water.

Although most B.C. fish are justly famous for their firm flesh, none can match the grayling. A freshly caught grayling feels like a bar of steel, and as an added bonus, it is one of the best eating freshwater fish, including such illustrious members as the rainbow and steelhead. Grayling have yet another distinction, as if they needed it. They do not have the characteristic odour of fish. Rather, the Arctic variety has a distinct odour of thyme. In fact this has led to its scientific name, *"Thymallus Arcticus."*

The grayling's mouth is quite small. In fact, the fish itself is not large. An 18-inch fish weighing a couple of pounds is considered a pretty fair grayling. I believe the world's record is only about five pounds, although I must admit I have never seen one even near that size.

The fish's diet is made up of insects and flies, together with underwater larva and nymphs. They spawn during May and June, usually on the clean gravel bottoms of fairly shallow rivers. In some areas there is lake spawning, apparently also on gravel. They do not construct nests. Their eggs are much smaller than those of trout, and they have an adhesive quality that binds them together in clumps.

With a little of the grayling's history and description under our chest waders, let us go out and catch a few. Grayling are found, as I have said, throughout the Arctic watershed, in most cases in streams and rivers. In this province they journey as far south as the Pack River, the scene of my first encounter. Peculiarly enough and for some reason I have never been able to determine, they travel no further south in this watershed. They first show up about mid-June, and remain for about a month. After that they move back out into the Parsnip watershed. Because of the nature of this river, most of the fishing is done from anchored river boats. As the waters drop, however, it is quite possible to take the grayling by wading the gravel bars, although here again a boat is necessary for transportation. Although our north country is opening up rapidly as new roads are being pushed further into what has been up to now virgin country, access is still a problem, and thus the need for a boat. The new forestry access road from MacKenzie up the Parsnip River crosses a number of good streams, although it sometimes takes a bit of a hike, as in most cases the best fishing is at the mouth of these streams. Further north, the Hart Highway parallels the Missenchinka, another good stream, particularly later in the summer and early fall. Some of the nicest grayling fishing I have ever experienced has been in the area of the Nation River, about 100 miles north of Vanderhoof on the Manson Creek-Germanson Landing road. This is the area of the famous, but short-lived, Omineca gold rush, and like that precious metal, grayling fishing is where you find it. A little stream, bubbling underneath the road or through a muskeg meadow, may appear absolutely fishless. But follow that stream down to the mouth, and in almost every case you are going to find a grayling. The prime requisites of angling for these fellows are a decent map, as large a scale as possible, a good pair of legs, and the necessary tackle.

This might be as good a spot as any to discuss grayling equipment. You can hook grayling on an almost endless variety of lures. I have had a 12-inch fish hit a big red-and-white Dar-Devl a third of its size. That occurred one fall while spinning for Dolly Varden in a back eddy of the Parsnip. It hit hard and fought like a little terrier. Light spinning lures work well at times, but as my friend Ken Melville says, it is almost sacrilege to use them. The real way to fish grayling is with a fly rod. Although the fish are not large, they do fight, and the cold water in which they live keeps them in fine shape. Fishing the small streams, a light seven- or eight-foot rod, balanced with the proper line, is the medicine. In the bigger rivers, the little rod is at times a disadvantage, but long casts are seldom necessary, and though you may at times have to make the little rod work harder than it should, the net result will be a lot more fun.

Grayling are not too particular as to flies, just as long as they are of a sombre hue. It is pretty well a toss-up as to wet or dry. For me, at least, the underwater variety seems to produce better in the earlier part of the season, although a hatch during the middle of a warm June day often requires a quick change. The various hackles work well—browns and grays—with the bivisible high on the list of my favorite dry flies. What is important is the size. The grayling has a small mouth, and the mouth is just about the only delicate part of the fish. Size 12 hooks are my favorite, with the odd No. 10 if the water is a

bit dark, as it often is in the spring. A supply of No. 14's can come in pretty handy. Surprisingly enough, and in spite of the fact that a large portion of the grayling's early season food is made up of larvae, I have had very little success with the very excellent nymph patterns available. It is an interesting subject; however, like most amateur fly-tyers, I still have hopes of someday turning out the sure-fire lure for my friend the grayling.

Leaders, of course, should match the fly size, although I must admit that most of the fellows with whom I fish prefer fairly stout leaders, say 2X. The sporting aspect has nothing to do with the choice, by the way. It is one of economy. Laying as they do close in to the willows, it is, at least in my case, more than easy to hang up. Usually a quick switch will break the fly loose, without loss. A slightly heavier leader will save many a fly, no little consideration when one fishes frequently. I have seldom found it necessary to use extra long leaders in this type of fishing, although I do think that the so-called "mist colored" variety, especially early in the season, seem to work a bit better than ordinary leaders.

Now how about the fighting quality of our quarry? Well, for one thing, a grayling very seldom jumps. A strike at a dry fly is more of a roll. The fish seem to arch out of the water and take the fly on their way down. Of course there is a fair amount of surface action, but most of the fish's fight is conducted in its own element. And there is a darn good reason too. The grayling knows the power of that big dorsal fin. Hook one on the edge of a strong riffle and heaven help you if it decides to turn sideways and put that big fin up. He is a canny little chap, and there are plenty of tricks and strength hidden away inside that steel-gray body. To further complicate matters, the grayling's particularly delicate mouth will not stand too heavy a rod hand. Try and "horse" a grayling, and you will be lucky to ever see him again.

At times they can be almost too easy, and then for no apparent reason will stop striking entirely. At times like that, you would think that every fish in the river had suddenly become afflicted with a mysterious disease and dropped dead. I had this experience a few years ago. We had nosed the big river boat into the willows, and as Ken was running the motor, it was my job to tie up. I have often thought my partner does this on purpose. With an uncanny bit of skill, that I have never been able to master, he seems to be able to put the bow in just far enough so that I have to do a bit of shoving to get a hold on a good branch. By this time, of course, he has already gone into action. That is the way it went on that first trip. Ken took a fish. I got untangled and picked up one, and then they quit. Ten minutes of casting and never a touch. "Well, Ken," I suggested, "looks like you'd better start that motor and we can try further down." Ken looked at me with the kind of expression he usually reserves for bait fishermen, and shook his head. "They haven't quit feed-

ing, just listen." All I could hear was the murmur of the river and the hum of insects, but finally I heard a strange sucking noise coming from the willows. "That," said Ken, "is a grayling." And darned if it wasn't. I could see the little fellow. Every few minutes he, or one of his friends, would sneak up to the surface and suck larvae from a branch, just at the waterline. Of course it was impossible to cast into that mess. However, as in most forms of angling, there were a few tricks I had not heard of.

Ken grabbed one of the long poles used for pushing a river boat through shallow water and without which no self-respecting river man would ever leave shore. At any rate, armed with the pole, he started to whale the very devil out of those submerged willows. I thought he had gone a little bush-wacky, until he explained. By his peculiar action he dislodged many of the underwater insects clinging to the branches, and of course, the grayling, ever ready to pick up an easy meal, followed the food supply carried by the moving water out into the open. It worked, too. We must have picked up another half dozen before somebody blew the whistle on our sport.

It is common knowledge that fish respond to changes in the weather, but it appears to me that grayling seem to be more affected by the elements than any other species of fish. It can be a beautiful June day, maybe a bit warm and oppressive, but with no hint of a storm. And those darn fish will quit and head for the bottom. If you happen to be a betting man and want a sure thing, lay down the price of a new fly line with your partner that there will be a weather change within a few hours, and you will probably win. As pointed out earlier, for spawning purposes, grayling require a supply of clear, cold water, and gravel. According to what little written information is available, unpolluted water is the only kind they will tolerate. Unsuitable conditions have already caused the extinction of the Michigan grayling. The hydro activity on the Peace, and the proposed activity elsewhere in the Arctic watershed, could well pose a threat to the existence of the Arctic grayling.

Having no commercial value, very little study has been undertaken on the species. Unfortunately, even if there had been, it is more than doubtful that any more consideration would be given to the ultimate fate of the grayling than is given to any other species of fish or game when large commercial or industrial interests are concerned. The fact is that because grayling do not have the public appeal of our more popular game fish, very few sportsmen will mourn their passing. A pity, really, because the fish embodies just about everything that most anglers are looking for. They can be taken on a fly, in a country that is as yet largely unspoiled. They can be difficult enough to tempt even the most jaded angling appetite. Oddly enough, they are a fish that many people have never even seen. For these reasons, if for no others, their loss, like the loss of any other of earth's inhabitants, would be a great shame.

However, perhaps it is inevitable, for many of the grayling's old companions have already disappeared. Fewer and fewer trappers roam our northern stream banks, and the old-time river men, who made those rivers their highways, have all but vanished. The blast of an air horn on some big highway transport drowns out the call of the loon, and old game migration routes are now replaced by black-topped highways.

There is a faint ray of hope. The grayling, like his old time companions, is a pretty tough character. In spite of what man may do to his environment, I would like to think that there will always be some quiet little back eddy, where the clean waters flood over gravel bars, and little clumps of half-submerged willows afford the protection the grayling needs. Hopefully, quiet streams, where the dark spruce come down to the water's edge, will always be with us. Perhaps they will be a little harder to find in the years to come, and the more precious because of that. But once found, such mysterious places will reveal, in their clear cold depths, the equally mysterious and colorful little fellow with the big fin, the Arctic grayling.

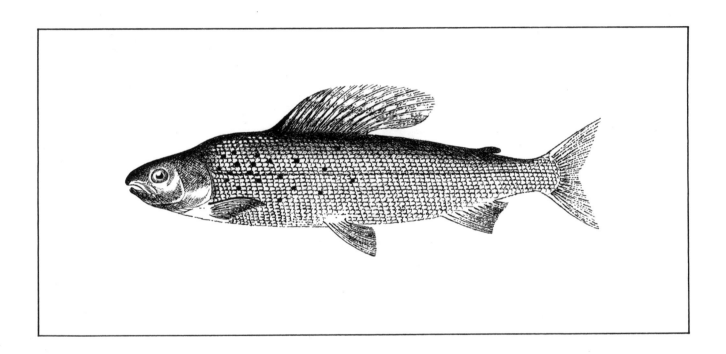

Dave Stewart

The Rocky Mountain Whitefish

ALTHOUGH we had been fishing for two hours, and although the fish we sought were actively feeding on salmon eggs, our bottle of store-bought salmon eggs remained practically full. The fish were calmly touring a clear, shallow run right at our feet. My father and I were fishing the Eagle River which flows into Shuswap Lake. We could clearly see several large Dolly Varden char and about 100 Rocky Mountain whitefish. Very occasionally we fooled a Dolly. But we couldn't fool the whitefish, and it was the whitefish we mainly sought.

The whitefish simply weren't interested in our drift-fished single salmon egg baits. What the whitefish *were* interested in was a pair of big coho salmon in a riffle immediately upstream of the shallow run. The salmon were spawning. The redd, or nest, had already been dug. The whitefish would inch upstream each time the cohoes settled over the redd. When the female coho skittered along the trench spewing her eggs, several whitefish would dart in behind her, pilfering as many eggs as they could before the scarlet-sided male drove them away. Sometimes a whitefish failed to dodge the male salmon's attack. We saw several crippled whitefish drift out of sight, twisting and rolling as they went.

Finally, I got impatient—and clumsy. As I shifted position, my foot struck the open bait bottle, which tumbled into the fast-moving water. The eggs quickly scattered in all directions. Muttering things he really shouldn't say in front of a 10-year old boy, my father retrieved the bottle and its few remaining eggs. Then he laughed (a little contritely, as I recall) and said, "Don't feel bad about it, boy. Those fish didn't like the blamed things anyhow."

His remarks seemed to bring on a startling result. The whitefish suddenly forsook the salmon for our preserved eggs. And there in the shallows, scant feet from shore, they quickly gathered up every last egg that I had spilled into the river. It was one of the most exciting moments of my early angling career.

I quickly dropped my bait into the melee, and instantly had a fish. My father did the same. For several minutes we caught fish right and left. Then we ran out of bait. Happily, my father already had a remedy in mind. He wasted no time cleaning the fish. Every fish gullet was crammed with coho salmon eggs; nearly every gullet had several of the preserved eggs I had kicked into the river.

When we finally stopped fishing—perhaps an hour later—we had all the fish we could carry home. At that time, the daily limit on whitefish was 25; there was no limit on Dolly Varden. I can't say whether we were within our limits.

Since that day many years ago, I have fished for whitefish throughout British Columbia. And although I have found them to be extremely unpredictable, I cannot recall a time when whitefish lost their minds so completely as they did on that memorable December morning of 1929.

Rocky Mountain whitefish are found in almost every stream of the province. They spend part of their lives in lakes, wherever lakes form part of the system they occupy. Accordingly, they are well known to anglers though often incorrectly labelled *grayling*, *chub*, or *squawfish*. In the glacial streams of the Selkirk and Rocky mountains, whitefish seldom exceed 10 or 12 inches. In streams of the Fraser system, where heavy salmon runs occur, whitefish attain their greatest size—often two to four pounds, but seldom more than 22 inches no matter what their weight.

Spawning takes place from late October through November, depending on water conditions. Redds are made in finer gravel and in slower and shallower water than used by salmon, but often within a few yards of salmon redds.

Whitefish are both desirable and challenging. They are probably the most numerous of our province's game fish, and unlikely to be much reduced by normal angling. In some areas—such as the Elk River in the East Kootenay —whitefish have been heavily fished for years, without apparent reduction. Because Rocky Mountain whitefish are both selective feeders and gentle takers, they are one of B.C.'s most difficult-to-catch fish.

Where they run in crystal-clear water—such as the Eagle River west of Revelstoke—they can be seen taking the bait. This makes it simple to set the hook at the proper moment. In less-clear water, or deep water, however, they must be feeding enthusiastically before a bite can be detected.

That whitefish are seldom caught by trolling is understandable; their habits simply make them unlikely candidates for trolled lures or baits. That whitefish have largely been ignored by flyfishermen is unfortunate because they occasionally do surface feed—on gnats, mosquitoes, and hatching larvae. At such times, they will rise beautifully to a dry fly. The fly must be selected and presented with much greater care than might be expected. Whereas rainbows and eastern brook trout will strike at flies which barely resemble their feed, whitefish will respond only to fly patterns which closely match their feed. Both the size and shape of fly patterns are of vital importance.

Generally speaking, No. 14 and No. 16 flies are necessary. Long, light leaders are a must. I prefer 5X or 6X leaders of nine feet or longer. The cast should be made almost directly onto the feeding fish—preferably from downstream. The take is always delicate: a tiny *slurp*, and a flash of silver. Whitefish hold the fly for a mere instant. And they don't hook themselves. Setting the hook is therefore a touchy but essential procedure.

When hooked on a light fly—or spin-fishing rod, the whitefish proves to be a game fighter. For the serious whitefish angler, a light spinning outfit is a must. It enables the fish to perform well, and it enables the angler to use sufficiently light sinkers and small baits. For most waters, a four-pound-test nylon monofilament line is ideal. Only two or three split shot are needed. The shot should be pinched onto the line about 16 inches from a short-shanked No. 8 bait hook. Single salmon eggs account for most of the whitefish taken from the Fraser watershed. Stone-fly nymphs, meal worms, or wood grubs are particularly effective when fishing the southern part of the province during the winter.

Although whitefish are generally tasty, the winter whitefish deserves particular praise. Like glacial stream whitefish, which are excellent pan-fare year-'round, the winter whitefish is usually far better table fare than summer or early fall whitefish. Smoked whitefish are also excellent. In my view, a smoked Little River whitefish closely resembles the Winnipeg Goldeye—a gourmet's delight.

To me, Little River whitefish are particularly interesting. Little River is a three-mile-long stretch of fairly fast and uniformly deep water. It flows from the main Shuswap to Little Shuswap Lake. Except for occasionally dry-fly fishing for them, I make one whitefish excursion per year. When I go after them, however, it is for a bunch, because I smoke them and want enough to make it worthwhile. My favorite time is March—when the fish are prime. And the most productive whitefish water I know in this province is the Little River downstream of Squilax Bridge. A fisherman can catch 50 or 60 whitefish there in short order.

In the past, Little River boasted seasonal abundances of Kamloops trout. During the spring, the trout entered the river in search of sockeye alevins emerging from the gravel of the river's spawning beds. A great hatch of stone-fly nymphs immediately followed the alevin emergence. Later, when the spring run-off swept yearling sockeye downstream, the trout again returned. And in the fall, when the sockeye spawned, the trout were once more on hand.

Coincident with the heavy trout runs came runs of whitefish. The whitefish were particularly interested in the stone flies and salmon eggs. But they were clearly secondary to the more aggressive and predatory trout. Moving from Kamloops Lake, these trout made an impressive sight as they passed near shore on their upstream migrations.

The heavy trout invasions continued through the 50's. Then the effectiveness of spinning gear became evident. As recently as 1958, the year of the big sockeye run, a

limit catch of heavy Kamloops trout could be taken from Little River in short order. These were mostly big fish too. I took seven- and eight-pound trout that winter, fishing with single salmon eggs.

The trout were noticeably smaller and fewer when the next big sockeye run occurred. That was 1962. In 1966, I had disappointing results. Insofar as accessible trout fishing is concerned, the Little River might still be termed good fishing, but compared to 10 years ago, it is nothing.

An interesting development occurred during the same decade. As trout numbers decreased, Rocky Mountain whitefish increased. The inevitable was happening: as man decimated the dominant species, a secondary species filled the vacated space. Nature abhors a vacuum. This may be a trite saying, but it remains true nonetheless.

The conclusion is mine alone. To my knowledge, no study has been made of the Adams-Little River whitefish. Nevertheless, it appears to me that those whitefish are becoming predacious. A large percentage of the whitefish stomachs I examined contained alevins. Several contained fingerlings. One large Adams River specimen (a four-pounder) contained a three-inch sculpin. It also had greatly enlarged jaws—all the better to swallow the relatively large mouthful.

I readily admit that my conclusions are based on a rather small sampling. I inspected dozens of fish; thousands should be studied. Similarly, the flies I used were tied to imitate alevin, fingerlings, or single salmon eggs. I might simply have been attracting an element of the whitefish population which was already inclined toward predation.

To conduct a valid experiment, it would be necessary to take seine-net samples the full length and width of the river. Before leaving the Shuswap country, I made tentative arrangements to do just that. It was to have been done *buckshee*. The Provincial Fish and Game Branch had no funds for such a project, but I was interested enough to do it on my own.

Someday, if the job is still undone, I think I'll have a go at it. I'm still very intrigued, and I keep thinking that the great inconnu of the north must have developed in a similar fashion—from an ordinary whitefish. And the inconnu, or sheefish (*Stenodus leucichthys nelma*), is the grandaddy of all whitefish. He weighs up to 60 pounds and measures up to five feet. (Inconnu are known to inhabit B.C.'s Teslin Lake and the Maskwa River.) If I stick around for a few milleniums I might see some mighty big whitefish in the Little River. Mind, I'd be careful not to confuse the new breed with the lake whitefish.

In 1923, the Dominion Government's Department of Fisheries introduced lake whitefish into several B.C. waters, including Shuswap Lake. The hope was to establish a winter fishery similar to that carried on in the other provinces. The project was dropped in 1927. No lake whitefish were reported taken, so it was concluded that they simply hadn't taken.

In 1958, while enjoying good spincasting for Kamloops at the mouth of the Adams River (I had beached several large trout), a particularly determined fish seized my bait, stripped out almost all my line, and then, when I braked hard, broke free. From its actions, I thought I had tangled with a large lake trout. I was rather miffed at being bested by a lake trout, so I switched reel spools, replacing four-pound-test line with 10-pound-test. Then I replaced my tiny bait hook with a No. 2 Viking, and baited this with a small strip of trout belly.

I cast into the outflowing river current, letting my new rig swing well out into the lake. Something tugged. I tugged back. For several minutes thereafter I wrestled with a hard-pulling fish which I felt certain was a laker, or grey trout as the Shuswappers call them. I was more than somewhat surprised when I slid a very silvery, broad-sided, eight-pound fish ashore. It was obviously a whitefish, but unlike any whitefish I had every caught. However, I was aware of the plantings of 1923-27. I simply concluded that my prize was a lake whitefish.

I gave it little thought till I happened to mention my catch to a biologist. He insisted that I was mistaken, and that I must simply have caught a large Rocky Mountain whitefish. He felt that it was highly unlikely that any lake whitefish had survived from the plantings. I got miffed all over again. Though I'm not a biologist, I've never had much trouble identifying fish. The upshot was that I went out and caught some more lake whitefish. I shipped several to Dr. C. C. Lindsay at the University of British Columbia. He thanked me for the samples, and verified my identifications.

Since then, I have taken lake whitefish at several places on Shuswap Lake. In addition to catching several at the mouth of the Adams River, I have caught them in Mill Bay across from Sicamous, off Scotch Creek, in the Narrows, and along the reef at the mouth of Blind Bay. All were taken in 30 or more feet of water, and all were taken on spinning gear. Several took a small Len Thompson wobbler—a No. 7 brass/red-and-white, I believe— and others took strips of fish, as did my first lake whitefish.

Lake whitefish, also called *common whitefish*, have been known to exceed 20 pounds. In B.C., most adult specimens weigh between three and five pounds. They are distinctive in appearance, having sharply-etched, large silver scales. In shape, they are more compressed than other whitefish, which gives them a flat-sided, hump-backed appearance.

Lake whitefish are native to lakes of the Yukon and Skeena river systems, and to some lakes in the Fraser River headwaters. And although they were introduced to many interior, Lower Mainland, and Vancouver Island areas, survivors have been reported only in the Shuswap, Arrow Lake, lakes of the Okanagan system, and Nicomen Slough on the Lower Mainland.

There are seven species of whitefish in the province of British Columbia. In addition to the three already mentioned, there are lake herring (or cisco), broad, round, and pygmy whitefish. Of these four, most are found only in the watersheds of the far north—in Teslin Lake, and in the Yukon and Liard-Mackenzie river systems. So far, they have received less attention than the mountain and lake whitefish. As the name suggests, pygmy whitefish are the smallest. They are usually less than six inches long. And pygmy whitefish are not likely to earn sportfishing praise. They are simply too small. But what is insignificant today may be valuable tomorrow. It is worth remembering that among a growing number of anglers the once-ignored Rocky Mountain whitefish are no longer mere curiosities. They have earned game fish stature.

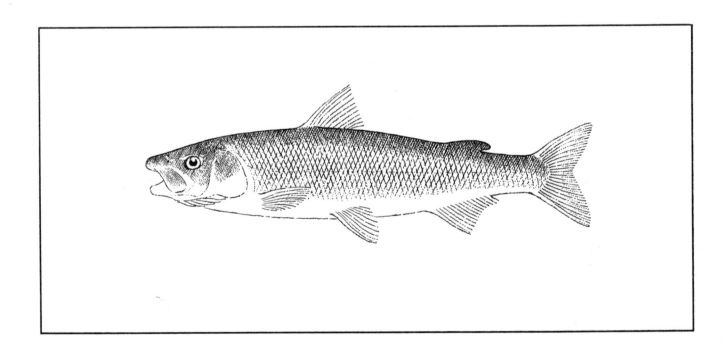

Pete Broomhall

The Pink Salmon

Aᴌᴛʜᴏᴜɢʜ it may be some time before the angling fraternity erects a monument to the pink or humpback salmon, nevertheless the pink is destined to become a truly important Pacific Coast sport fish. And, quite apart from his sporting qualities, the pink is an interesting fish.

Of the five species of Pacific salmon, the pink has the shortest life span, is the smallest at maturity, has the fastest growth rate, is the least dependent on freshwater, has the most protein, and is probably the most prolific.

The pink's birth-to-death cycle is completed in just two years. At maturity, pinks average about five pounds, and that weight becomes quite significant when compared to the weights of other two-year-old salmon. Even the growth rate of the mighty spring sometimes seems abysmal by comparison; two year-old springs frequently weigh less than one-quarter pound.

Whereas springs (and cohoes and sockeyes for that matter) often spend one or more years in freshwater before migrating to the sea, pinks (and chums for that matter) leave freshwater almost at birth. And this early migration to the sea of plenty is the main reason for the pink's rapid growth rate.

It is fortunate that the pink is a prolific salmon. It could even be argued that the primary reason for the pink's growing status as a sport fish is his numbers. Sooner or later, the steady decline of the spring and coho salmon populations would have obliged sport fishermen to look favorably on the small and long-ignored pink. Even if other salmon populations do not continue to decrease, the steady increase in the saltchucker population means that the sport catch will have to be more and more widely distributed. Under such circumstances, the discovery of any new sport species is always welcome.

The pink's sporting qualities were discovered relatively recently. Newly-effective lures and fishing techniques have proven that he is not always a lure-shy fish. And the advent of spinning and other light-weight saltwater tackle has made it possible for the humpback to perform on a par with his larger and more coveted brethren.

Although pinks can be caught every season, the angler who does so must travel in alternate years. And this is because, for some inexplicable reason, north-coast rivers have their best runs on even-numbered years, and south-coast rivers on odd-numbered years.

On alternate years, rivers of the respective areas have poor runs. And because pinks are invariably two years old at maturity, the two-year, good-run-bad-run pattern never changes. The town of Courtenay on Vancouver Island seems to be the division point between north-coast and south-coast patterns.

If fisheries' biologists are successful in transplanting pinks from one watershed to another, we may one day enjoy good pink runs every year—in both the north-coast and south-coast districts.

Pink salmon fry leave their freshwater birthplace almost as soon as they emerge from the gravel. When they arrive at the sea, they are less than two inches long.

During the seaward migration, these small silvery fry attract considerable attention from cutthroat trout. (Hence pink salmon fry are indirectly important to the river and estuary trout fisherman.)

Soon after they reach the sea, the young pink fry disappear. They reappear in the summer of their second year. In the early summer, they are silver bright, and during this stage in their short career, pinks are often mistaken for coho or spring salmon.

The veteran sea fisherman can often identify the pink from its fighting qualities; the less experienced may even mistake a boated pink. As a general rule, a quick glance at the tail is usually enough. If the tail is covered in blotches, the fish that belongs to the tail is a pink. But, if the tail is all over spots, the fish is a spring. The trick is to tell blotches from spots.

If there is still doubt, the pink has very small scales, and the interior of his mouth is very white; springs have larger scales and black mouths. Naturally, the best way to learn the difference is by comparison. After catching a few of each species, the differences become very evident. Incidentally, there is no need to mistake pinks for cohoes; a coho's tail is very sparsely spotted, and what few spots there are occur at the wrist of the tail, on the dorsal surface.

As far as the sportfisherman is concerned, the pink is most desirable in his sea-bright state. To get the most from pinks—both in appearance and in fighting qualities—the saltchucker is advised to meet the salmon when they first appear at the estuaries of their parent streams. Mid-August is perhaps the safest time. Soon after that, the pink loses his sea-silver sheen.

Of course there are exceptions; some pink salmon runs occur far earlier and some far later. But the aim is still to meet them when they are at their prime. As maturity overcomes him, the pink quickly darkens—thus reducing his appeal. Also the males (and only males) soon develop pronounced humps on their backs (which helps to explain why the name *humpback* is often used to describe this salmon, but does not explain why male sockeyes—which also develop a considerable hump—are not also so named).

Although pinks are taken on a variety of lures, and by a variety of methods, many sea fishermen refuse to use heavy tackle when fishing for them. The small but sporty salmon is at his best on either light trout spinning gear, or on fly-fishing tackle. Furthermore, when conditions are right, the spin or flyfisherman can frequently outperform his heavier-tackled brethren. Perhaps this is largely because pinks tend to school-up as their return migration

carries them close to their parent stream. By choice and habit, spin and flyfishermen tend to anchor amid, or to drift among the schools, rather than to troll through them. And, clearly enough, the longer the line is in the vicinity of salmon, the greater is the fisherman's chance of scoring.

The light-tackle enthusiast is further assisted by the fact that pinks are none too secretive about their whereabouts. They often fin right at the surface. And when the run is at its peak, there is no mistaking their presence. The passing of a school is often both audible and visible.

But locating the salmon is only half the battle. One must also pick an appealing lure. And this is not so easy as it might appear. Of the many lures and flies that might well be pink-getters, very few are highly valued by the experienced pink-salmon seeker. Perhaps the two most popular are the Hotrod and the Deadly Dick. Each should have a touch of fluorescent pink or red, and each should be fished with painfully slow retrieves.

The uninitiated may be surprised to learn that pink salmon do not really strike. They merely accept lures. And, because their mouths are softish, it is not really

necessary to set the hooks. One needs only tighten into the fish.

The slow-retrieve technique is partly based on the fact that the lure must often be well down before it will be effective. This even applies when pinks are cavorting at the surface. For some reason or other, the surface pink is often reluctant to take. Perhaps the lure sinks too quickly, and is soon lost from sight. Perhaps the deeper fish have a much better and longer view of the fluttering lure. Or, perhaps, the surface fish only *seem* reluctant. It might simply be a comparative thing; there might be more fish in the depths than at the surface. Whatever the reason, it is often wise to fish the lure both slowly and deeply, even when the pinks are busily frisking at the surface.

The experienced pink salmon fisherman also tries to anticipate the movements of the small salmon. His main aim is to identify the direction in which the school is moving. Then he casts ahead of the school, allows his lure to flutter down, and slowly begins his retrieve. Fished slowly enough, the weight of the Hotrod or Deadly Dick is usually enough to sink the lure to where the fish are. Seldom does a spin fisherman have to use additional weight.

The flyfisherman's technique is much the same as that described for the lure fisherman. He also aims ahead of the school, pauses, then slowly retrieves. But the fly-fisherman's best opportunities occur when the pinks are both right at the surface and in a cooperative temper. Quite naturally, the flyfisher often elects to use a floating line which keeps the fly buoyed near the surface where it can be readily seen by surface-finning pinks. The top-rated flies, like the favored lures, have touches of flourescent pinks or reds. Some popular patterns are the Umpqua, Red-and-White Streamer, and Pink Shrimp.

Like other Pacific salmon, the pink seems to be responsive to both light and tide. Sometimes a school (particularly a river-mouth school) will show during the early and late hours—or for brief periods during a tidal change—then disappear completely. On such occasions they have often merely sounded. And on such occasions, the lure or fly must also get well down if it is to be effective. Under these conditions, the flyfisherman is somewhat disadvantaged.

But, if a lure fisherman has to wait for his offering to sink to the appropriate depth, the flyfisherman only has to wait longer. The impatient flyfisher may find a high-density sinking line a decided asset, particularly in deep water. But such flyfishers soon discover the disadvantages of using high-density lines in only moderate depths. A

Hi-D line simply cannot be retrieved slowly enough among the bottom-hugging pinks. It keeps getting snagged (on the bottom, of course). A medium-density line is usually more practical. It may take longer to sink, but it allows the necessary slow retrieve.

As time goes on, it is inevitable that more and more sea fishermen will seek the pink. And more pink salmon haunts will be discovered. Presently, there are only a few recognized locations. The mouth of Indian River at the head of the North Arm of Burrard Inlet is probably the best known spot.

Depending on the viewpoint, it does and doesn't matter that the Indian River is so close to Vancouver. Up until about a dozen years ago, not too many saltchuckers knew or bothered about the Indian River pinks. Since then, crowds have made the discovery. On many weekends (of odd-numbered years), both the head of the inlet at Wigwam Inn and the creek-mouth at Granite Falls would be crammed with boats.

Some of the assembly were obviously on hand to snag fish. Although snaggers used conventional rods and reels, they did not use conventional terminal tackle. (Isn't it the same even today?). They favored large treble hooks and heavy sinkers, and they retrieved the lethal gear in sharp jerks through a school of fish. Invariably there was a jerk at both ends of the line.

Others of the assembly knew how to take the pinks legally—and some of them consistently outperformed the snaggers. In those days, limits were commonplace, and often enough several fish would be hooked simultaneously.

As a rule, fishermen are a friendly and humorous lot—until they are forced to rub elbows with one another. Then, lines and tempers often become crossed. It was no different at Indian Arm. There were many cooperative and humorous incidents. There were also near-homicidal incidents, and even some of a larcenous nature. For example, a tired, line-attached pink might pass too closely to a luckless angler. And because the true owner of the fish often did not know precisely where his fish was amid the grand boatjam, he would seldom see it being quietly netted. Once in a while, however, the hi-jacker was caught red-handed. He would then spend some anxious moments fending off an irate boarding party.

With such keen competition, one had to devise very specialistic techniques in order to compete. A little boldness went a long way. So did some white lies. But not insultingly barefaced lies. For example, you wouldn't lie to a neighbouring caster about your lure. Hell no, he could too easily spot the lure you were using. But, if he was not wise to the aforementioned slow retrieve, you could blame your success on a number of red-herring reasons. You might even act just plain dumb, as well as dumbfounded: "Well, now, ain't that strange—another of them hunchback fishes just grabbed my spoon again."

Or, you may want to make furtive motions in the bottom of your boat, as if dipping your lure into some secret potion. The main purpose of the Brer Rabbit technique is to keep the opposition confused. It's all part of the friendly game of one-upmanship, like scattering weed seed on the lawns of angling competitors a week or so before the pinks are due.

Until about ten years ago, all this nonsense—and some excellent fishing, too—occurred at the mouth of Indian River. Since then, the Indian Arm pink salmon fishery has waned sharply. Log-booms now cram the head of the inlet, and pinks are far fewer in number. Unless there is

a sharp improvement, it would probably be wise to search much farther afield for less-contested salmon. Fortunately, there are still bays, creek-and river-mouths where good pink salmon fishing can be enjoyed.

One such spot is just north of Campbell River on Vancouver Island. It is a smallish bay fed by a very small creek. It is also particularly suited to flyfishing. The pink salmon have usually assembled there in fair numbers by mid August (on even-numbered years). It is then possible to expect reasonable sport either from a boat or by wading the estuary foreshore at low tide.

While their condition lasts, pinks can be expected to please both the angler and the gourmet. But, as the season progresses, pinks quickly become more colored and less desirable. It is then time to leave them unmolested, and to dream of future encounters.

Harry Lomax

The Lake Trout

I CAUGHT my first lake trout about four o'clock on a sunny September afternoon. It was a rather lacklustre experience. It could even be called a let-down. I had worked hard and suffered many insect attacks to get that fish, and when I caught it, I wasn't much impressed.

Since that sunny September afternoon, nearly one quarter of a century has passed. And during those intervening years, I have learned to respect the lake trout. I leave the scoffing to others. For me, there is no doubting that the lake trout is a worthy game fish.

The term *lake trout* is really a misnomer. The fish is actually a char, *Salvelinus namaycush.* The char is also known as Great Lakes char, grey trout, Mackinaw trout, salmon trout, and laker. The lake trout of Maine is called togue. The lake char of British Columbia is one of the two chars that are native to the province. The Dolly Varden is the other. The lake trout is closely related to both the Dolly and the eastern brook trout. The latter fish, also a char, has been introduced to several B.C. lakes and streams.

The British Columbia lake trout is found from Shuswap Lake northward. A single specimen, the only one ever reported from farther south, was taken from Okanagan Lake in November, 1969. It weighed 39 pounds.

Lake trout are not found in every lake north of the Shuswaps. They require cold water, and although they can tolerate water to 65 degrees Fahrenheit, they prefer water from 40 to 50 degrees. During summer, the preferred temperatures can consistently be found only in the larger, deeper lakes. And when lake trout are deep, it usually takes wire line and heavy sinkers to reach them. Considering that most lake trout are taken with that sort of heavy tackle, it is little wonder lake trout have been branded sluggish fighters. Even a steelhead would be hard pressed to perform against such tackle odds.

Lake trout are better able to prove themselves during the spring and fall. They are then in shallower water and can be taken on conventional spinning tackle. Even so, they seldom put on the spectacular aerial display of a salmon or trout. Perhaps this is because lake trout are too smart to waste energy jumping out of their natural element. Instead, they make deep, surging runs, and do a whole lot of head shaking. Both tactics can put severe strains on the angler's tackle. And the battle is not over when the lake trout is brought to the surface. That feat is usually nothing more than the end of the first round. Chances are excellent that the laker will sound again, which begins round two. The angler is often obliged to tease his prize surfaceward several times. The heavier the fish, the more rounds he lasts. And more than one tired fisherman has been thankful that a lake trout does not include aerial acrobatics in his bag of tricks.

Some lake trout, of course, simply don't abide by the rules. I recall one in particular. I met him at Steamboat Bay on Trembleur Lake. Trembleur is one of the lakes comprising the Stuart-Trembleur-Takla watershed. In addition to lake trout, each of these lakes contain rainbow, kokanee, and whitefish. And since they are large lakes, it takes some knowledge to find the best fishing areas. Steamboat Bay has long been one of the better-known spots.

It was nearly lunch time when my partner and I noticed a flurry of activity just off the mouth of a small creek. We had been trolling slowly toward shore—to have lunch —or we might have missed it. We quickly cut the motor. Then, as we drifted closer, we prepared our spin-casting gear. We had no idea what breed of fish was making all the rucus. On the first cast, a 10-pounder took. The water at that point was only five feet deep. Naturally, the fish could not bore downward. He took the other option. In fact, his jumping display so resembled a rainbow that we were surprised to discover the fish to be a lake trout. What made it all the more improbable was the fact that it happened in the middle of a hot summer day. According to all the theories, no self-respecting lake trout had any business being within a mile of the spot. The unusual number of fry in the area led my partner and I to conclude that the lake trout had probably followed the smaller fish from deeper water. In any event, for a short period, we enjoyed truly fantastic fishing.

Like the Dolly Varden, the lake trout has an excellent appetite. I've caught them on largish lures when they were so gorged they seemed incapable of swallowing anything larger than a gnat. Lake trout principally feed on smaller fish—including whitefish, kokanee, coarse fish, and very possibly trout and char. They will also take aquatic insects, field mice, lemmings, and even young ducks and young muskrats.

Despite their seemingly insatiable appetite, however, lake trout are not always easy to catch. Though intense, the feeding periods are often very brief, and the periods vary considerably from area to area on any given lake. Then, too, there's the lake trout's distinctive strike. Many anglers experience considerable difficulty in hooking lake trout simply because they do not understand how the fish feeds. The strike usually feels like a heavy bump, as if the lure hit bottom. The lake trout usually attacks his victim from the side, disabling it; he then engulfs it head first. For this reason, when a char is not hooked securely on the initial strike, the lure should be dropped back, then quickly brought forward. This tactic will often tempt a lake trout to strike the second time. And because the char has a big, bony mouth, the angler should do *his* striking with considerable force.

It is worth noting that the lake trout's bony mouth is generously supplied with large, very sharp teeth. These teeth make the removing of hooks a rather delicate operation. For this reason, pliers should be used, and before

the operation is attempted, the fish should be completely exhausted or very dead. In addition to the danger presented by the laker's teeth, there is the problem of dealing with a strong big fish. It is not particularly wise to grab blindly at a big, thrashing fish of any kind. I once had the unpleasant task of removing a treble hook from the palm of an unhappy angler who had not yet learned the lesson.

The weight of lake trout varies considerably, not only from lake to lake, but also from area to area on the same lake. I have found certain holes that seem to hold only large fish—20-pounders—while several nearby holes clearly hold far smaller fish. The "nursery" holes usually occur in shallower water. The only explanation I can offer is that the large fish take over the best feeding areas, driving out the smaller lake trout. I have seen more than one char bearing marks that could only have resulted from the toothy attack of a much larger specimen.

Although the lake trout of British Columbia probably average 10 pounds, they attain weights of 50 to 60 pounds. And although the lake's size does not seem to govern the lake trout's size, the lake must have sufficient depth. The largest lake char I have seen taken from Babine Lake—a huge lake—weighed less than 20 pounds. A nearby and relatively small lake, Cunningham Lake, regularly produces lake trout close to 30 pounds. Francois Lake west of Prince George has a large population of six- and seven-pounders, but few over 15 pounds. The much smaller Cluculz Lake, also west of Prince George yields a fair number of 25-pounders.

In choosing lake trout fishing tackle, there are two

main considerations: the size of the fish, and the season of year. During the summer months, it is virtually impossible to do much with light spinning tackle. Except in the most unusual circumstances, a spin-cast lure simply cannot reach the required depth. Nor can a light spinning outfit adequately handle the heavy sinkers and large lures used in the deep trolling that is so necessary during summer. Light spinning gear comes into its own during the early spring and fall. I have occasionally taken small char on a fly rod, but I don't recommend it. In addition to the strain it puts on a valuable rod, a lake trout's deep run is difficult to handle on a light rod. A fairly stout spinning rod is probably the best all-round choice. It should be fitted with a substantial spinning reel and 15-pound-test monofilament line. Such an outfit will perform adequately both for fairly deep trolling and for near-surface spinning.

Lake trout can be taken on a wide variety of lures, but the larger lures are by far the most popular. Wobblers such as the F.S.T. and Gibbs Stewart are good producers in most areas, as are flatfish plugs. I have had particularly good results with flatfish during September—when the kokanee are spawning. However, I prefer lures which have a less violent action, and which therefore put less strain on a light rod. Because a lake trout's teeth are dangerous to both line and angler, many fishermen use short wire leaders between line and lure.

Since lake trout are not triflers, it is wise to carry either a strong, salmon-sized net or a long-handled gaff. Lake trout of 15 or more pounds are not casually flipped aboard. I once boated a large lake trout by hand, but I'll never attempt such a stunt again. At boatside, the fish appeared to be completely played out. I grasped it firmly behind the gills—in the same manner salmon or trout are often treated. All went well till I had the fish half out of water. Then, the hook fell out, and the fish came back to life. And it wasn't my fish. Even worse, it was my companion's first lake char. He was understandably anxious to boat it.

Somehow my grip held, and somehow I managed to wrap my free arm around the fish. This put the char's toothy mouth about one foot from my face. It was probably my imagination, but I do believe the char chose that moment to growl at me.

With lake trout, gilling can also be dangerous. Gilling calls for slipping a finger or two under the gill plate before the fish is hefted. But lake trout are often deeply hooked. And the idea of encountering a set of hooks somewhere in the gill area has never appealed to me.

The lake trout of B.C. are primarily lake dwellers. I have taken a few from rivers and streams, but they were always only a short distance upstream from a lake. The lake-dwelling habit sets the lake trout apart from the other chars. Both the Dolly and the eastern brook trout are found in many streams of the province.

At one time, the char might have been a marine fish. In his *History of Fishes*, J. R. Norman points out that char originally were centered in the Arctic Ocean. They gradually established fresh-water colonies in lakes throughout much of the northern hemisphere—as far south as Switzerland. But it isn't necessary to look back into history to discover that there are many mysterious things about the lake trout. To me, the young lake trout is still a mystery. Despite having spent years fishing throughout central B.C., I have yet to catch a truly small lake trout. The little fellows must be somewhere, but where they are, and what they feed on, I have yet to learn.

Lake trout are one of the few species of game fish that have been successfully hybridized. The *splake* is the result; it is a cross between lake trout and brook trout. Splake have already been introduced into some lakes in B.C.'s Kootenay and Yoho National parks, as well as selected lakes in the vicinity of Vancouver. I have seen

the splake of the Canadian Wildlife Service's Jasper Park fish hatchery, and I am told both that they apparently grow to a fair size, and that they can tolerate higher water temperatures than the lake trout. In lake stocking programs of the future, such a tolerance might be an important consideration.

Like all species of char, lake trout spawn in the fall—from mid-September to early December, depending on the area. But unlike other char—or salmon and trout for that matter—lake trout do not require running water for their spawning. They normally spawn on rocky reefs or on gravelly bottoms of lake shallows.

Although I like the lake trout at any season, I have a particular fondness for the fall lake trout. On more than one occasion, they have added a welcome dimension to a fall moose hunt. And fall lake trout are fat as hogs. No doubt their prime condition can be related to the fact that they face a long winter. To me, prime-conditioned fall lake trout are also outstanding table fish.

In my view, the best-eating lake trout is a baked lake trout. When I do the cooking, I simply remove the excess fat from the body cavity, fill the cavity with poultry dressing—all same stuffing a chicken—rub a little cooking oil over the skin, place the fish in a roasting pot, and pop it into the oven. When I barbecue a lake trout, I wrap the fish in foil instead of using the roasting pot. Served with new potatoes and fresh green peas, a lake trout is certain to tickle the palate of the most discerning gourmet. However, a word of warning: if the barbecuing is conducted outdoors, the fish must be large enough to feed several neighbours for the essence of baking char is certain to attract guests.

Anyone who has caught and eaten one prime lake trout quickly forgives the fish for not performing in the same spectacular fashion of the steelhead or rainbow. Anyone who has caught several lake trout on reasonable tackle knows they need no forgiveness; he knows theirs is a game, if different battle. And anyone who has frequently fished for lake trout knows that there are many dividends to the sport; he knows that the quiet places are still the best places, and he knows that many of the better lakes still possess all the wild beauty of an unspoiled land—birch-lined shores, sandy coves, sparkling water, the eerie early-morning call of the loon. Across such a lake, somewhere, in the deep water off a steep bluff, a big lake trout is waiting.

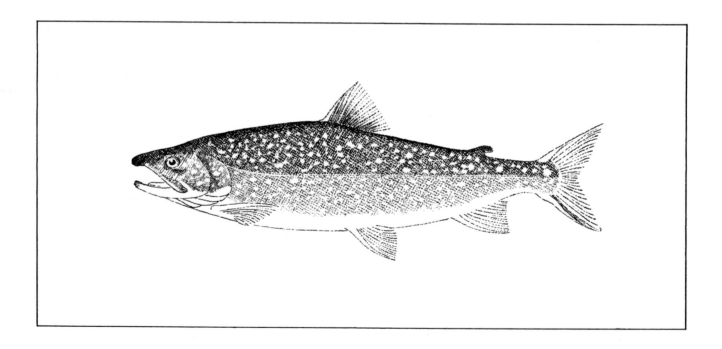

Dave Stewart

The Dolly Varden

A CRISP OCTOBER day was making its golden exit some- where beyond Trout Lake when Nelson sportsman Jack Martin and I stopped at the log-jam. It was a big log-jam. It clogged the entire Lardeau-Duncan River. The sun's last yellow rays cast eerie shafts down through the twisted logs. We peered down. The shifting current gave us intermittent glimpses into the depths. Almost immediately we caught sight of a huge wavering form. We spent the next few minutes watching. Sometimes we could see only a head or a tail; sometimes we saw the entire fish.

I believe that Jack may very well have caught fishing fever that day. After making several futile attempts to drop his spoon where the big Dolly Varden could see it, he turned to me.

"Okay, smart guy—*you* try it."

I was quite ready to do just that. This was a new game to Jack, but I'd been yanking Dollies out of log-jams for as long as I could remember. I waited for the right instant, then dropped the spoon. It lit close to where the big head was hidden by logs. Making a quick turning loop, the Dolly grabbed the spoon, and shot back into hiding.

I knew I only had time for one good pull. I reefed hard, and kept reefing. But before I could drag the threshing form clear of the logs, the leader parted. Back went the biggest fish we'd seen all day.

"You *had* him. He won't bite again, will he?"

"Not on a spoon, he won't. That's certain. But I'll show you something about Dolly Varden."

With that I scrambled shoreward over the slippery cottonwood logs. In a few minutes I scrambled back with a 10-foot maple pole, wrist-thick at the butt. I tied the largest single hook in my kit—a 6/0 from a Gibb's Dia- mond—to a piece of cuttyhunk which was my ever- present cure for everything from ripped trousers to split canoe paddles. On the hook, which hung about six feet from the tip of the hefty "rod," I impaled a strip of belly taken from a Dolly we had caught earlier. Jack nearly split his sides laughing at my gear. I ignored him, and quietly manoeuvered the ungainly mess into position. I had to wait several moments for the right opportunity. When the swirling waters shifted toward the big Dolly, I dropped the bait.

I wasn't really too hopeful. A hooked fish is a wary fish, even if that fish is a Dolly. But fresh meat is very attractive, even to a recently-hooked Dolly. Out he shot, grabbed the offering, and turned back toward safety. I heaved hard. The maple stick bent double. With a great splashing, the big fish came up. For an instant, he caught against a log, then I had him out of the jam. And even as I heaved, I was galloping across the greasy logs to shore.

Jack quickly came over to view the red-spotted, broad- sided 30-inch fish. He had stopped laughing, but I could sense a lot of questions forming in his mind. After, all I

103

had been extolling the virtues of light tackle, especially dry flies, all day long. Yet here I was employing the crudest of tactics. I reassured him:

"You understand, of course, that I seldom do this sort of thing. But I thought you might be interested in seeing how some people fish for Dolly Varden."

As a matter of fact, I haven't resorted to that sort of thing since that day. But even that far back, in 1955, the Lardeau-Duncan Dollies were diminishing rapidly. Spinning gear and greatly increased fishing pressure were the causes. But, at that time, I thought little of it. Early teachings are hard to unlearn. When I was a boy, there were neither bag limits nor closed seasons for *Salvelinus malma;* the Dolly was the bad boy of the game-fish world. He was accused of ruining trout and salmon populations, and "true sportsmen" often killed and discarded any Dolly they caught. In some areas, bounties were even offered for Dolly Varden. Happily, there has been a change in the past two decades.

In most British Columbia waters, Dollies are hard scrappers. True, they seldom break water. But then, neither do their highly-touted cousins, eastern brook trout. And although I've had several Dollies that jumped like rainbows, I'm not disappointed with the char's more normal deep-boring and hard-pulling fight. And a prime Dolly can pull just as hard as any trout or salmon.

Dolly Varden were once held in low esteem largely because so many anglers caught poor-conditioned fish. With Dollies, such a mishap is understandable. Dolly Varden spawn during July, August, or September, depending on the watershed they inhabit. Since most Dolly fishing used to be done during these months, a large percentage of those taken were lank, flabby snakes of fish with pale, watery flesh, elongated teeth, and hooked jaws. Today, more fishing is done during late fall, winter, and spring—when Dollies are in good condition.

A prime Dolly Varden is a fine-looking fish. Two- and three-year-olds tend to be big-headed and flat-chested, but they quickly fatten after becoming big enough to prey on whitefish and kokanee. Their first year of heavy feeding usually occurs in deep water. As they reach adulthood, their bodies deepen, their heads cease to look oversized, and their colour becomes more pronounced. The yellow spots on their flanks become flame orange. The fins become two-toned, ranging from pale to dark orange and contrasted by a ribbon of white along the leading edge. It is interesting to note that the spots of eastern brook trout are similar, though haloed by blue and somewhat redder in shade. Dollies of the north coast and Trout Lake (north of Lardeau) often have wavy markings

similar to those found on the eastern brook. The spawning Dolly is very bright. The flanks are flame orange; the bellies, fins and spots are deep red. Males are usually far more brightly coloured than females.

In addition to being a good fighter, the full-bodied Dolly Varden is also an excellent table fish. The bright orange flesh has the delicate, tantalizing flavour common to the Dolly's close relatives, the Arctic char and eastern brook trout. Slabs of Dolly Varden, toasted brown over alder coals, are nothing less than gourmet food.

Dolly Varden occur in B.C.'s four main watersheds: the Fraser, Skeena, Columbia, and Peace. They are also found in most coastal rivers and lakes, and in streams along both coasts of Vancouver Island and the Queen Charlottes. Most of the glacial streams along the Selkirks and Rockies contain dwarf Dolly Varden (often misnamed *brook trout* or *mountain trout*). These fish seldom exceed 12 inches, and are both very slender and very pale. In the larger, non-glacial streams along the west slope of the Rockies, Dollies are often very large. Twenty-pounders have been taken from the Wigwam and Flathead systems.

Of all B.C. game fish, Dollies are by far the most enthusiastic biters. In fact, they are very susceptible to overfishing. They're always on the prowl—even when well fed. And they will amost always take a well-placed bait or lure. Because they are overly cooperative, they are becoming downright scarce in many streams. They are especially vulnerable during the spawning season. At that time, they become just plain silly. I recall catching several recently-spawned Dollies on strips of blue pasteboard cut from a matchbox.

Even prime Dollies can get overly enthusiastic. A few years ago, while living in Revelstoke, I took my four sons on a mid-June Dolly fishing trip to Crazy Creek near Taft. Our struggle through the heavy brush was quickly rewarded. In short order we landed several two-pounders. While son Gary was looking for a safe place to land one such specimen, it suddenly and irresistably returned to the depths. Gary was unable to see what had caused the turn of events, but from my perch on a high rock, I could. A huge Dolly had simply seized the two-pounder crosswise in his jaws, then calmly swam away.

The large fish finally opened his mouth—probably to get a better bite—and Gary retrieved his quite dead fish. But the big cannibal wasn't through. He swirled close behind the departing victim, nearly scaring Gary out of his wits. We all then disregarded the lesser fish still lurking in the pool. Dave finally hooked the monster, and after a 15-minute battle, beached it. At 32 inches, it was the largest Dolly I had ever seen in Crazy Creek.

104

Crazy Creek is a clear and icy tributary of the Eagle River. At one time, many other Eagle River tributaries had good runs of Dolly Varden. The same was true of nearly all the many creeks feeding Shuswap Lake. Because of the big char's reckless acceptance of baits and lures, and because of the wanton slaughter of spawners, the Dolly Varden populations are now greatly reduced. And the surviving Dollies are also much smaller than those of the past. A few decades back it was relatively simple to literally load the boat with five- to 20-pounders. Some are still caught today, but few reach five pounds.

The Shuswap situation is not an isolated case. Until fairly recently, many big Dollies were taken from the Columbia River near Revelstoke and Arrowhead. These fish were almost as large as the Kootenay Lake giants which spawn in the Lardeau-Duncan. When the kokanee left Arrow Lake for the spawning streams along the Columbia, the Columbia Dollies followed. The Dollies fed on the little redfish. Prior to World War II, 20-pounders were often taken at the mouth of the Tum-tum, the Jordan, and the dozens of creeks up the Big Bend. Today, the Dollies still follow the kokanee run, but they are now far smaller and far less numerous.

It will be interesting to see what effect Mica Creek Dam will have on the Columbia's game fish. It may even prove to be beneficial. The dam will stabilize water flow, and settle out the glacial silt which clogs the water each summer. And although the flooding of spawning streams may more than offset any such benefits, spawning channels can be built to counteract the loss of spawning

grounds. If such measures are adopted—and they should be—we may yet see a resurgence of the great Columbia River Dolly runs.

The same applies to the Kootenay Dolly Varden which depend on the Lardeau-Duncan for both their spawning and their autumn forage. But if counter measures are not taken, Kootenay Dollies will suffer further setbacks.

There is very little recorded information regarding the Dolly Varden. That anglers of yesteryear had a low opinion of the Dolly did not help. Nor do I agree with all the information that is available. For example, I take exception with part of the Dolly's description given in the otherwise excellent handbook *The Fresh-water Fishes of British Columbia*: "body troutlike, but long and slender, with large head . . . ." The remainder of the description is accurate, but the quoted portion describes either an immature, or a recently-spawned fish. A mature Dolly in prime condition is as heavy for his length as the average trout. There are exceptions, of course. Dollies and whitefish are often the only fish hardy enough to live in the glacial streams of the mountainous areas of the province. And, naturally, where "pickin's are slim," the Dolly is apt to be "long and slender, with large head . . . ."

In the large lake-and-stream systems, however, there is no doubting that the Dolly Varden thrives. And although they may spend a large portion of their lives in streams, there is no doubting that Dollies do best where they have access to large lakes.

Dollies spawn in small tributary creeks that are both cold and pure. And they spawn much earlier than most salmonids. They usually enter the small streams early in June, six or more weeks before spawning. In these confining waters, they are vulnerable to anglers, and especially vulnerable to the poacher's spear or gaff.

After spawning, Dollies slowly make their way downstream. It may take them several weeks to return to the lake (or large stream) from which they began their spawning migration. After reaching their home lake, they more or less stay put. They seem to favour the area adjacent to the mouth of their own nursery stream.

I have had the opportunity to observe Eagle River Dolly Varden for many years. These fish spend much of their early years in the river. They spawn in various tributaries to the Eagle—Yard Creek, Gorge Creek, Crazy Creek—and in several small streams adjacent to the four mountain lakes that comprise the Eagle's headwaters. Several clear streams feeding the North Fork also support Dolly runs.

During most of the summer, small Dollies can be found in the small tributary streams. Then they disappear, returning eventually as mature spawners. During the intervening three or four years, they often take up seasonal quarters in the Eagle River. They now range from two to three pounds, and have the lean, large-headed look.

A few of these lean fish accompany the fat, mature fish on their early summer migration into the spawning creeks. Others of the lean type appear when the kokanee spawn during late August and early September. Some stay right through the salmon run, returning to Shuswap Lake in December. In January, Dollies again appear in the Eagle. The January Dollies are on hand in anticipation of the soon-to-emerge kokanee alevins. Many of them are quite large. By March, most of the Dollies have dropped back to the lake, where they can be caught by spincasting near the rivermouth.

At one time, the classic (and thoroughly illegal) method of catching Dolly Varden called for a small trout as bait. Since most of the creeks where Dollies spawn contain either cutthroat or rainbow, it was simple enough to obtain the bait. The bait was impaled on a No. 2/0 bait hook. Because heavy leaders and stout cuttyhunk line were used, finesse was at a minimum. A hooked Dolly was simply ripped from his element and flung onto the rocks.

Today, the majority of Dolly Varden are taken on spinning lures. The Dar-Devl type of wobbler (or any similar red-and-white wobbler) will take Dollies in most waters. Small plugs, flatfish, and devon minnows also work well. Salmon eggs are excellent bait during the autumn and early winter. No matter what tackle he uses, however, it is obvious that the angler of today has considerable respect for the Dolly Varden.

The new respect is manifest in a curiosity about and concern for the Dolly. The attention directed toward searun Dollies is fairly typical. Because Dollies in the sea lack colour, they are sometimes moderately tricky to identify. However, shortly after being taken, the tell-tale yellow spots usually begin to show through the silver. My experience with searun Dolly Varden is limited. I've taken a few from the Campbell River and Tofino-Ucluelet districts on Vancouver Island, and from the Deena and Copper Rivers on Moresby Island. Most weighed about one pound; none exceeded two pounds.

Until recently, Dollies were abundant in Fraser Valley streams. I have caught them up to eight pounds near Hope, but I doubt that they were searuns. From reliable witnesses, I have heard of large searun Dollies in the coastal streams of northern B.C. If so, they are probably a subspecies of the searun char. I base this conclusion on the fact that extensive studies of the searun Dollies of Alaska show that full-weight searuns seldom exceed three pounds.

The interest shown by Alaska is heartening. It shows an about-face regarding Dolly Varden. From 1922 to 1941, various bounty programs were undertaken in Alaska. The programs were aimed at eradicating or reducing "this predacious menace to red salmon." Finding the bounty method ineffectual, Alaska tried other measures. The overt abuse ended when biologists decided that *Salvelinus malma* took fewer salmon fry than had been supposed, and that the the eggs they took were usually free drifting anyway.

Russian biologists have also been studying the Dolly Varden. Up to 1958, they had repeatedly urged control measures. Then, in 1960, a report by K. A. Savvaitova categorically stated that it was "impossible to consider char solely as predators deserving of elimination. Char . . . may exert a harmful influence on populations of *Oncorhynchus nerka* (sockeye) by destroying their young. Nevertheless, it is impossible to assume that *all* forms are harmful in all waters. On the contrary, in many cases char are useful in that they destroy small, useless plankton eating fishes, as was shown earlier by F. V. Krogius and E. M. Krohkin. In reducing the abundance of char . . . we create conditions favourable for the development of food competitors of those salmon whose young remain in fresh water for a prolonged period. As a result, their (the salmon fry) feeding conditions are made worse . . . ."

The Alaskan studies show that searun Dollies spawn during October and November. A single female may deposit as many as 6,000 eggs. The female digs the nest unassisted. The male keeps busy by fighting. The eggs hatch four to five months after being deposited. During their first three years, the young Dollies grow very slowly. They spend most of their time feeding along the bottom of their nursery stream, usually hidden from sight under rocks, logs, and overhanging banks. The seaward migration occurs in the third or fourth year, at which time the Dollies average about five inches. After their first seaward migration, Dolly Varden commence a pattern of migrating to and from lakes, spending winter in the depths of lakes and returning to feed in the ocean during the warmer months.

Dolly Varden that originate in non-lake systems must locate a lake in which to spend winter. The Alaskan studies indicate that this is accomplished through random searching. However, when the time comes for them to spawn, they unerringly return to the stream of their birth.

Most searun Dollies spawn at age five or six. About

50 percent live to spawn a second time. A small percentage spawn three or more times. Mortality is far higher among males than females, and few of either sex live beyond eight years.

It is generally believed that all B.C. Dolly Varden belong to the species *Salvelinus malma*. However, since at least one other species has been located in North America (the *Salvelinus alpinus* of Alaska), since Japanese biologists recognize two species, and since Russian biologists describe a total of 16 species and subspecies, it seems highly likely that two or more species occur in this province.

But no matter how many species there are, and despite his previous poor press, it is certain that the Dolly Varden of British Columbia rightfully deserve a place among the province's game fishes.

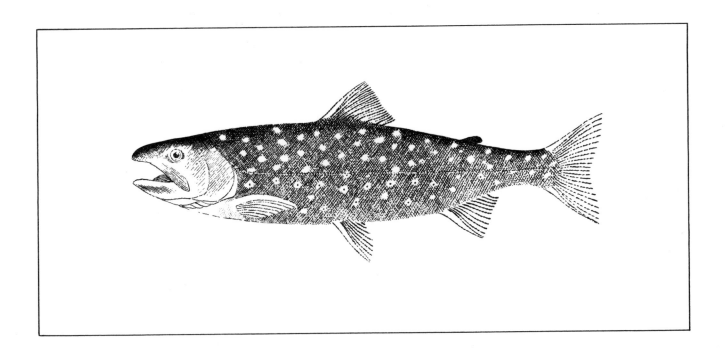

Forthcoming books in the
Western Fish & Game outdoor series:

British Columbia GAME ANIMALS
British Columbia GAME BIRDS
The British Columbia FLYFISHER
The British Columbia RAINBOW
British Columbia SEARUNS